FLAVOURS OF THE STREET

TURKEY

Hande Bozdoğan

Photographs by Ahmet Tozar

TIMES EDITIONS

Managing Editor: Jamilah Mohd Hassan
Editor: Lydia Leong
Designer: Ang Lee Ming
Production Co-ordinator: Nor Sidah Haron

© **2004 Marshall Cavendish International (Asia) Private Limited**

Published by Times Editions — Marshall Cavendish
An imprint of Marshall Cavendish International (Asia) Private Limited
A member of Times Publishing Limited
Times Centre, 1 New Industrial Road, Singapore 536196
Tel: (65) 6213 9288   Fax: (65) 6285 4871
E-mail: te@sg.marshallcavendish.com
Online Bookstore: http://www.timesone.com.sg/te

Malaysian Office:
Federal Publications Sdn Berhad (General & Reference Publishing) (3024-D)
Times Subang
Lot 46, Persiaran Teknologi Subang
Subang Hi-Tech Industrial Park
Batu Tiga, 40000 Shah Alam
Selangor Darul Ehsan, Malaysia
Tel: (603) 5635 2191   Fax: (603) 5635 2706
E-mail: cchong@tpg.com.my

National Library Board Singapore Cataloguing in Publication Data

Bozdoğan, Hande, 1965-
Turkey / author, Hande Bozdoğan; photographer, Ahmet Tozar. – Singapore : Times Editions, c2004.
p. cm. – (Flavours of the street)
Includes bibliographical references and index.
ISBN : 981-232-699-5

1. Street vendors – Turkey. 2. Vending stands – Turkey.
3. Snack foods – Turkey. 4. Cookery, Turkish.
I. Tozar, Ahmet, 1964- II. Title. III. Series: Flavours of the street

TX360
641.3009561 — dc21   SLS2004006556

Printed in Singapore by Tien Wah Press (Pte) Ltd

CONTENTS

ACKNOWLEDGEMENTS

The making of this book was spread over a period of almost two years, with numerous field trips across Turkey, substantial library research and long interviews with a wide range of people, from street sellers and chefs to housewives skillful in the kitchen. It is not possible for me to remember and list them all. Nonetheless, with my sincere apologies for any unintended omissions, I would like to thank the following people:

My first and foremost thanks go to Ahmet Tozar who has been part of this project from its inception to completion, not just as the professional photographer but also as my co-traveller in this journey into Turkish culinary culture. In exhausting field trips and studio shootings, he always invested his expertise and dedication with great generosity and humour. The project became a learning process for both of us and above all, we had fun together (except when he ate the baked rice puddings before photographing them!)

My sister Sibel Bozdoğan made invaluable contributions to the shaping of this project, edited the final manuscript and gave me much needed encouragement. I will always cherish not only the experience of working with her, but also all the memories of good food, family cooking and culinary capital that we shared over the years (including the recipes we exchanged over expensive overseas telephone calls).

Long before I embarked upon a career in the culinary arts, my mother, Necla Bozdoğan, taught me the pleasure of home cooking and the importance of a tasteful dinner table. For these and much more, I am grateful to her. As for the hard-earned joy of professional cooking, I thank all my teachers and colleagues in the French Culinary Institute in New York. The training I received there gave me new insights with which to approach the material in this book.

Mahasti Kia did a superb job with photography editing during the production of the manuscript. (Our only disagreement arose when she suggested using her Photoshop skills to doctor the street photographs and eliminate the cigarette butts in order to give a cleaner and more presentable image of Turkey!) I owe her many thanks. The same goes for photography assistant Eren Engin who shot some of the field photographs; to Yeşim Akşirin who did the reproduction photography and to Hüseyin Ortak for his help during the photograhy sessions at night.

My special thanks go to Hasan Övet for all the driving he did for this project and for his special trip to the Black Sea coast to bring me chestnuts and corn flour; to Ali Osman Kapan, a talented corporate cook in Istanbul for helping me handle the calf liver; to Filiz Hösükoğlu in Gaziantep for her much-appreciated help in introducing me to the intricacies of southeastern cuisine; and to the staff of Kolaylar Manav (my grocery store in Arnavutköy, Istanbul) and especially to young Seçkin for supplying me with the best fruits and vegetables.

During my search for a publisher, Zuhal Elver gave me invaluable PR advice and Zeynep Ataman of Gamma Medya generously shared her experience. I am grateful to both of them. Thanks are also due Joan Eröncel for copy editing the manuscript and checking my English before submission.

Finally, I thank Kaya Didman, along with Latte and Zoe, for eating my culinary creations with such an enormous appetite and with such obvious joy that words were unnecessary; I knew that I could take all the chewing and gulping as a big compliment. It is my hope that the reception of this book will give me a similar sense of accomplishment and pride.

Hande Bozdoğan
April 2004
Istanbul

INTRODUCTION

One of the most fascinating and unique aspects of Istanbul, admired by many visitors to this great world city, is the variety, richness and quality (not to mention the cheapness) of foods one can purchase in the streets. In busy intersections or urban squares, itinerant vendors sell their appetising wares in hand-pushed carts or glass display cases on wheels or simply, trays or baskets that they carry from one spot to the next. These culinary delights range from fresh produce (like seasonal fruits and vegetables) and popular items that are constant traditional features of Turkish urban life (such as *simit*, a kind of round sesame bagel) to prepared meals (like stuffed mussels or rice pilaf with chickpeas). The men who sell these foods are themselves fascinating subjects of urban ethnography, most of them migrants from rural areas, residing on the urban fringes of Istanbul and struggling to make a living in this so-called 'informal economy'.

Even more fascinating is the fact that such street-based culinary trade is the continuation of centuries-old commercial practices in Istanbul. In his history of Istanbul in the second half of the 17th century, Robert Mantran observes that, judging from the amount and variety of fresh produce, meat and other foods entering and circulating within the city, Ottoman Istanbul was, first and foremost, an insatiable centre of consumption.[1] He lists lamb meat, dairy products, rice, fresh fruits and bread as items of highest consumption and adds that the wealthier sections of the population also consumed substantial amounts of fish, poultry and eggs. Mantran also notes that numerous vegetable gardens existed around the villages along both shores of the Bosphorus, citing the artichokes of Ortaköy and the cucumbers and cabbages of Kadıkoy among others. Another prominent historian, Reşat Ekrem Koçu, talks about street foods in particular, giving us a vivid picture of the variety and sophistication of prepared foods that were available in the streets during the Ottoman Empire.

Itinerant cooks selling stew? (Istanbul Metropolitan Municipality, Atatürk Library)

He mentions various stews of beans, chickpeas, courgettes (zucchinis) and potatoes, and writes that numerous itinerant cooks specialising in soups, rice and couscous could be seen in the streets, catering primarily to construction workers.[2]

Historical records also testify to the meticulous control the state exercised over these trades, especially those using meat and grains, the basic staple foods for the city's vast population. The cleanliness of the pots, the amount and kind of meat that should be used for meat pastries *(böreks)*, the exact required weight of breads and quality of particular dishes and desserts were all specified in detail by successive regulations.[3] Underweight breads, insufficiently cooked meats or spoiled foods were heavily fined. Different regulations were in effect for different trades such as butchers, dairy producers, sherbet sellers, pickle sellers and yoghurt sellers.[4] According to 17th century chronicler Evliya Çelebi, the practice of regulating prices goes back to the reign of Mehmet II whose grand vizier Mahmud Paşa went on regular rounds to inspect the prices of fruits and vegetables in the markets. A document from 1680 also mentions fines for selling and purchasing food items in locations other than the designated market areas.[5] Reading about these historical precedents, one cannot help thinking how little the relationship to the state or the municipal governments has changed for many of today's street sellers. It is not uncommon for any visitor to see a street seller running away from municipal inspectors, lugging his cart behind in a frantic escape. Most likely, he does not possess the necessary permits for selling his wares in a particular location or he sells something that does not conform to the specified standards of quality and hygiene. When caught, he may have to pay a hefty fine or worse, his cart may be confiscated, but almost invariably, he will be back on the streets in a few days. Selling food and beverages in the streets is the primary and only means of livelihood for thousands, and more often

Carts of fresh fruits and vegetables, Adana

than not, the inspectors will turn a blind eye in the case of less serious offenses in this familiar cat and mouse game.

There is no question that in today's Turkey, life is increasingly harder for street sellers. Some of these centuries-old practices are rapidly becoming obsolete, following shifts in patterns of food purchase, preparation and consumption unleashed by the phenomenal proliferation of large supermarkets and fast-food chains in Turkey since the 1980s. With globalisation, advertising and television creating new habits and aspirations typical of contemporary consumer societies everywhere, entire urban populations are shifting their grocery shopping increasingly more to large international supermarket chains like Migros or Carrefour, driving many small corner grocery stores out of business. Compared to the latter, street carts and itinerant vendors still maintain some advantage in this competition because of the cheapness and convenience they offer to their customers, not to mention the absence of overhead costs like store rents. Nonetheless, many of them are also threatened or are at best marginalized by the emerging trends in conspicuous ways. Although the purchase of certain basic items (such as fresh fruits, vegetables and fish) from the street is still a common practice across the entire social spectrum, many other kinds of street food, specially prepared or ready-to-eat items (such as pastries or fried fish) are consumed mostly, and in some cases exclusively, by the poorer sectors of the urban population today.

In addition to changing tastes and aspirations, tougher standards of hygiene are also partly responsible for the progressive disappearance of certain types of street food. In the last 20 years or so, the public is far more health- and hygiene-conscious and the government is eager to catch up with Western standards. A famous example is the still-contentious fate of stuffed and grilled lamb intestines *(kokoreç)*, one of the most popular street delicacies that is

Fresh fish, Urla, Izmir

threatened by Turkey's bid for EU membership. Another manifestation of these new regulations can be observed in the case of cotton candy *(pamuk şeker)* or wafer discs *(kağit helva)*, nowadays required to be sold in clear plastic wrap. Finally, in a rapidly transforming and modernising society like Turkey, it is the changing aspirations of the street sellers themselves that is most likely to bring a decisive end to many of these traditional practices. A good many of the sellers featured in this book see themselves as the last generation in their trade, accepting with a mix of melancholy and pride, that rather than continuing the family business, their children will probably get a higher education and/or a 'proper job'.

First and foremost, this book is a tribute to these disappearing traditions. The idea for it originated a few years ago in my desire to document some of those 'street foods' representative of an historically established but rapidly disappearing urban culture with its particular flavours, colours and smells that make up an important part of my childhood memories. Some of the items that I have set off to document are no longer sold in the streets (such as yoghurt); others have disappeared in the course of the preparation of the book (such as the gooey street candy *(macun)* that was already obsolete during my field trips, with the exception of a rather token *macun* seller in Izmir who was more of a tourist attraction than the familiar figure of my

A coffee house owner taking a break, Kilis

childhood) and still others have continued to thrive and will probably do so for a long time (such as *simit* or fresh fruits and vegetables). Before everything else, I wanted to capture what is unique about these street foods. The most important for me is their seasonality—the unrivalled 'luxury' of eating strawberries in the right season (spring), with their 'real' taste, or experiencing the distinct seasonal rituals of making jams and preparing pickles. I became particularly aware of this in New York when I first encountered the seasonless hothouse strawberries—bright red, photogenic and fascinating at first, but without a memorable taste, flavour or fragrance. They made me realise the subtle sense of time, seasonality and locality that I associate with food in Turkey—a country where the experience of each of the four seasons is very distinct unlike many places in the tropical belt (without real winters) or in the northern climates (without real summers). While appreciating the convenience of working with ingredients available throughout the year, I also remembered that familiar feeling of anticipation when certain dishes could only be savoured in certain seasons—how, for example, my mother's delicious chestnut cake *(kestaneli pasta)* or leeks in olive oil *(zeytinyağlı pırasa)*, one of my all-time favourites, meant winter, and could not be eaten at any other time. These thoughts led me to arrange the material in this book in a loosely seasonal sequence, as a way of conveying some sense of the associations between particular foods and particular months of the year.

Secondly, and perhaps as significant as their seasonality, is the mobility of street foods; rather than going grocery shopping, the groceries come to you, delivered to your door by the itinerant vendor. Many Turks still cherish the convenience of buying, say, peeled and sliced pumpkins by just calling out of their windows or down from their balconies to the cart below—a convenience that is increasingly rarer to come across these days. Especially in traditional Turkish neighbourhoods where typically men bring the daily groceries and women hardly ever venture out of the neighbourhood on their own,[6] itinerant vendors of fresh produce, water, *simit*, bread and such items bring much-needed goods and services to women's home-centred domestic lives. To appreciate the significance of this mobility, readers are invited to pay

Fresh greens in season

attention to the carts, baskets, trays and portable stands of the street sellers featured in this book—especially their ingenious designs, functionality and decorative treatment. There is something primitive but also enchanting about such portable stalls and ornate carts used extensively to sell almost everything—not just street foods, but also a wide range of fascinating items, from toys and clothing to colognes and cheap fragrances. Evocative of a snail or turtle carrying its house on its back, these 'miniature stores' mounted on wheels or collapsible legs give the beholder some sense of what street commerce must have been like before the advent of modern shops.

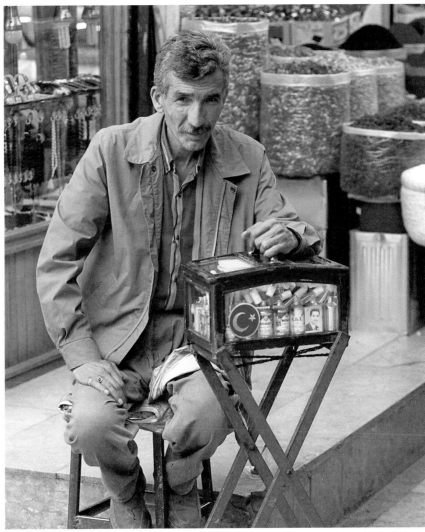

Cologne, fragrances and essential oils, Gaziantep

Thirdly, the individual stories of the itinerant vendors and the familiarity that develops between them and their regular customers distinguish the purchase of street foods from the anonymity of the supermarket experience. In stark contrast to modern supermarket shopping, buying and selling in the street is not an abstract, impersonal transaction between anonymous agents, but rather a little bit of socialising, a little bit of therapeutic complaining (about the weather, the prices, the politicians, various ailments, etc.) and a little bit of commerce all at once. For example, it is very common for a melon seller to seek advice from a customer who happens to be a doctor or a lawyer, or to alert a favoured customer to the arrival of a particular kind of melon that he or she likes. To the extent possible, this book tries to incorporate the individual stories that reside behind each one of these street sellers, to present them not as 'human vending machines' but rather, as real people with real lives, problems and aspirations.

Then there are the moods and settings. Through the photographic documentation of the street sellers, this book tries to convey the profound sense of beauty embodied in these urban

Heading home after a long day

fragments—the harsh but romantic nocturnal rounds of the seller of a fermented millet beverage *(boza)* on cold winter nights, the mysterious glow of the *burma* desserts in a glass display case hit by the setting sun, or the melancholic sight of a lonely cart, still waiting patiently for the last customer when dusk descends on empty streets at the end of the day.

Finally, I have also tried to capture the unschooled but remarkably sophisticated aesthetic sensibility that often goes to the presentation or display of the street foods. With their textures, smells and colours, these food items offer a sensory feast to the eye and many sellers are extremely skillful in using this to their advantage. From the eccentric fresh fruit seller in Adana who stacks his apricots and peaches in perfectly neat rows to the cotton candy seller in Istanbul whose colourful display is a work of art in itself, itinerant vendors constitute a unique urban aesthetic that this book seeks to preserve.

Spice and produce market, Antakya

The actual making of this book took almost two years and the initial concept evolved in the course of this process expanding outwards from Istanbul to cover other regions of the country. Successive research trips revealed that while the cities of Eastern Turkey and the Black Sea coast were relatively poorer in terms of the variety of street foods one could find, it was in the southeast, the Mediterranean and the Aegean that many culinary treasures could be discovered. Hence, along with Istanbul, Ankara, Izmir and Adana as the four largest cities in Turkey, the cities of the southeast (Antakya, Gaziantep and Urfa in particular) are also heavily represented in this book. There seems to be an obvious climatic rationale to this regional distribution: street life is far more active and colourful in warmer climates and street foods tend to flourish in such places.

Items featured in this book cover a very wide spectrum, from generic street foods that can be found everywhere (*simit* is again the classic example) to obscure local specialties specific to a region (such as the *mırra* coffee of the southeast). Although each item's region of origin is specified in the text and the captions,

Map of Turkey

it is not the regional distribution but rather the seasonal sequence that has determined the organisation of this book. At the same time, the reader should note that although the four seasons are very distinctly experienced throughout Turkey, exactly when a season starts and when it ends varies greatly from region to region. For example, the southeast and the Mediterranean coast enter summer much earlier than other parts of the country and summer foods and fresh produce from these regions feed the populations of Istanbul, Ankara and other northern cities before their local produce appears. Likewise, the famous artichokes *(enginar)* sold in the streets of Istanbul come from the Aegean region first and only later in the spring, from the local gardens around Istanbul. With this in mind, the seasonal classification of the material in this book should not be taken as designating an absolute overlap between certain items and particular seasons. Rather, it should be read as a loose classification to give only a general sense of characteristic tastes, colours and moods associated with a particular season.

While the documentary project evolved, the aesthetic and culinary potential of the material was too tempting to resist in my professional capacity as a chef and I decided to incorporate some recipes into the book. Inspired by the items one can purchase in the streets of Turkey, I compiled a recipe collection of popular and practical dishes representative of traditional tastes and well-established culinary practices. In this, I relied not only on extensive library research and existing cookbooks, but also, and perhaps more significantly, on my own accumulated culinary experiences and on the personal knowledge, favourite dishes and recipe notebooks of three generations of women in my family, along with a wide circle of friends and neighbours. The recipes featured in this book—these 'translations' of popular street food into more sophisticated gourmet dishes—are my personal selection from this compilation, all of them reinterpreted with a more contemporary culinary style and tested carefully in my kitchen prior to being written up and photographed. The same standards of professional excellence and aesthetic perfection that went into the field photography were also applied during the shooting of these dishes in a professional studio. In the end, what you are looking at is not just a 'coffee table' book featuring Turkey's street sellers with artful photography, nor a conventional 'cookbook' to be used as a source for recipes, but rather a combination of the two—a thematic cross-section of Turkish culinary culture.

Street market, Urfa

While the increasing sophistication and cultural diversity of culinary books in the international market in recent years is a sign of the expanding interest in such material, Turkish cuisine is often subsumed under the general category of "Middle Eastern food" (largely limited to meat dishes), missing all the subtle variations, regional differences and lesser-known tastes (especially of vegetable dishes) unique to it.[7] More focused thematic volumes, such as this one concentrating exclusively on street foods, are almost entirely non-existent. With the aim to fill this lacuna, this book is intended for a wide international audience, from seasoned travellers and cooking enthusiasts interested in culinary cultures of the world, to general readers interested in Turkey and Turkish culture. It hopes to take the reader on a colourful journey through Turkey and to the extent possible, to appeal to all the senses of the reader as if he or she is actually touching, tasting and smelling the items featured in the following pages.

WINTER

Although street commerce decreases conspicuously during the coldest months, it never ceases completely, and winter is not without its own characteristic colours, tastes and rituals that redeem this harsh season.

With the exception of the Mediterranean where winters are milder, Turkey is typically cold and snowy from late November well into March. The damp cold can be bitter in Istanbul and the amount of snowfall has increased conspicuously in recent years. Street life diminishes in intensity, and eating and drinking mostly recede indoors. People seeking warmth and refuge from the elements tend to socialise indoors, where the sound of little spoons stirring glasses of tea can be heard or cups of warm milk drink *(sahlep)* are served with cinnamon sprinkled on top. At night, sellers of a fermented millet beverage (*boza*, sold exclusively on winter nights) roam the empty streets, yelling out their arrival to the people indoors. Hearty soups become indispensable starters for meals, especially chicken broth, lentil soup and the traditional Turkish *tarhana* soup—a powder of vegetables and dry yoghurt, prepared during the summer for winter consumption. Other indispensable items of winter cuisine are jams, pickled vegetables, sun-dried tomatoes and chillies, all of which preserve a taste of summer even in the coldest months.

Although street commerce decreases conspicuously during the coldest months, it never ceases completely, and winter is not without its own characteristic colours, tastes and rituals that redeem this harsh season. Roasted chestnuts become a standard fixture of street corners, smoking over makeshift grills and giving out a welcome sense of warmth even before one actually holds them in hand. Quinces and bananas, which are mostly unavailable in other seasons (although imported bananas have changed this fact in recent years), are distinct and eagerly anticipated tastes of midwinter, especially in desserts, jams (quince), cakes and shakes (banana). Winter vegetables like cabbage, celery, leeks, carrots, spinach, onions and potatoes fill the street stands and markets, to be used for stews, soups and other humble but delicious winter dishes of the common folk.

Fish is consumed in almost every season in Turkey, but the best catches come in cold winter months and fish markets overflow with turbot, sea bass, blue fish and most famously, *hamsi* (fresh anchovy), a small fish specific to the Black Sea. Most of the fish sales take place in the evening when people rushing home are attracted by the variety and freshness of the fish. Most of the time, wherever there are fish stands along the sidewalk, other street sellers also accompany, offering whatever else may go with a fish dinner, especially lemons, spring onions (scallions), turnips, carrots, lettuce and rocket *(roka)*.

Street scenes in winter. Opposite, clockwise from top left Floating fish restaurant, Eminönü, Istanbul; Itinerant orange seller, 1903 (Postcard, author's collection); Pickle cart; Roasted chestnuts

QUINCE *Ayva*

In midwinter, quince sellers can be spotted in the streets of Istanbul and other major cities. Typically, they carry a large basket on their backs; a few ripe yellow quinces, their green leaves still attached to the stems, are decoratively displayed on sticks around the edge of the basket. Since quince is a fairly heavy fruit, the quince seller cannot fill his basket to the brim (especially if he is an old man as they usually are) and the money that he can make in a day by selling what he can carry is usually a meagre sum. Old postcards and engravings offer evidence that this manner of selling quince in baskets is a centuries-old tradition in Turkish culture. Given the fact that many other fruits far more common than quince (such as apples and oranges) are not sold in this particular manner anymore, one wonders why this tradition has persisted for so long. There is no doubt that quince is a special fruit with a considerable history behind it.

In terms of its texture, quince is a difficult fruit to eat; the uninitiated may find themselves choking on it. (This is the source of the common idiom *ayvayı yemek* ("eating the quince") which designates a person in a difficult and miserable situation.) The sellers often make a point of warning customers that it has to be chewed well and not hastily swallowed. The particular variety also makes a difference; a ripe and succulent quince offers an exquisite eating experience. Among many different varieties of quince, the *aromatnaya* quince is cited by sources to be the most suitable for eating fresh, along with the tender yellow fruits of the *smyrna* quince.[1] The etymological root of the word "quince" is traced to *"kudonion"*, Greek melon or "Apple of Cydonia", a town in Crete long famous for growing quinces. It is essentially a fruit of the eastern and northern Mediterranean; the mythological "golden apple" awarded to Aphrodite by Paris for her beauty. Although a very popular fruit in medieval and Renaissance times, culinary histories record that the quince declined in popularity in later periods, perhaps due to its hard texture and the long time needed to cook it thoroughly. More recently, immigration from the eastern Mediterranean to Europe and the United States has made the quince popular again in the West.[2]

There are countless uses of quince in Turkish cuisine— among others, jam, marmalade, compote and a very popular baked dessert *(ayva tatlısı)* eaten with clotted cream. Most of the time, shopping for the quince takes place in the market but the occasional quince seller in the street is still a very interesting feature of the contemporary urban landscape. The story of Hasan Turgut, one of Istanbul's many quince sellers today, is fairly representative of the many similar lives sustained by selling fruits in the streets. Originally from Konya, a central Anatolian town, Hasan migrated to Istanbul, following his father and uncle who had also been quince sellers. He brings his quinces from the Adapazarı region, some 120 kilometres east of Istanbul. When the quince season is over, he switches to selling plums, peaches and other seasonal fruits. Although he sells the latter on a wheeled cart that he parks in one street all day, he carries his quinces from one street to another in a large basket, not knowing exactly why he continues this exhausting tradition. He lives in Eminönü at the tip of Istanbul's historical peninsula, and he walks to the streets of Şişili and Nişantaşı, some six kilometres away, carrying his heavy burden on his back.

It is a popular belief in Turkey that an abundance of quince in a particular year is a sign of a cold winter to come. When I asked Hasan Turgut if this was true, he responded: "All these years, I have never noticed!"

Quince seller catching his breath during a break, Istanbul

Quince Tart *Ayvalı Tart*
(Serves 8)

Ingredients

Sweet Pastry Shell

Plain (all-purpose) flour	250 g
Icing (confectioners') sugar	50 g
Butter	150 g, cut into cubes
Egg yolks	2
Vanilla essence (extract)	
Cold water	1 Tbsp, if needed

Filling

Quinces	7
Lemon	1
Granulated sugar	110 g
Ground cinnamon	1 tsp
Ground cloves	1 tsp
Water	100 ml
Butter	1 Tbsp
Apricot jam	4 Tbsp

Method

- To prepare the pastry shell, put all the dry ingredients in a bowl then add butter. Work with your hands until the texture is sandy. Add the egg yolks, vanilla essence and drizzle with water if the dough is too dry. Work into a smooth dough, trying not to overwork.
- Roll the dough very thin, brush the excess flour on both sides and place into a 25 cm diameter fluted tart shell with removable bottom. Chill in the refrigerator for 15–20 minutes.
- For the filling, peel and core 4 quinces, then cut into 1–1.5-cm cubes. As you proceed, keep the cubes in lemon water to avoid any discolouring. Put the cubes into a pot with the sugar, ground cinnamon, ground cloves and water. Cook until the pieces are tender but not mushy.
- Peel, halve and core the rest of the quinces. With the help of a mandolin or using a sharp knife, slice into 2 mm thickness. Again, keep the slices in lemon water as you go.
- Remove the tart shell from the fridge, spoon the quince cubes into the tart shell, filling it up to three-quarters high. Pat dry the quince slices and arrange them fanned, on top of the quince cubes, generously overlapping as they will shrink while cooking. Brush the top with melted butter and bake in a preheated oven at 175°C for 40–45 minutes, until the edges of the quince slices are golden brown.
- Put the apricot jam in a pot with equal amount of water and bring to the boil, stirring until there are no lumps. Brush the top of the baked tart with this glaze carefully.
- Wedges of the quince tart can be served with a scoop of vanilla ice cream or whipped cream.

Roasted chestnut seller, Istanbul

CHESTNUTS *Kestane*

When chestnut carts start appearing on the sidewalks, winter is imminent. Different varieties of chestnuts (some smaller and rounder, others larger) are roasted on simple coal stoves. When they are done, the chestnuts are kept warm on the edge of the stove, waiting to be packaged in different sized paper bags for a range of prices. Once in a while, a chestnut peeled in hungry anticipation may reveal a dark, rotten inside: what a disappointment! For eager consumers who devour the chestnuts on the spot, another problem is disposing the shells when there is no trash bin in sight. In recent years, resourceful chestnut sellers have resolved this by offering an extra paper bag.

The etymological history of "chestnut" is believed to go back to the Greek *"kastanea"*, meaning "nut" from the region of Castanea in Pontus, the northeastern shores of Asia Minor or possibly the region of "Castana" in Thessaly, Greece. Another possible origin of the word is the Armenian *"kaskeni"*, passing into Latin as *"castanea"*. For centuries, this ancient fruit and the majestic trees upon which it grows have populated different regions of the Mediterranean and Asia Minor.

Today, in many cities of the world, roasted chestnuts are an unmistakable sign of urban life in winter, from a busy street corner in Manhattan to a crowded ferry landing by the shores of the Bosphorus. In Istanbul, whatever one happens to be doing on a particular winter day—window shopping, going to the cinema or watching the seagulls circling above the passenger ferries under a blanket of snow—chestnuts are always there to warm the hands as well as the heart. It is as if the city is more liveable and more magical because of chestnuts. For the locals and visitors alike, the sight and smell of roasted chestnuts is a treat in itself, not to mention the musical ring of the chestnut seller's voice filling the cold air: *"Kestane kebap, yemesi sevap!"* ("Roasted chestnuts, blessed is the one who eats them!")

Chestnuts are also luxury ingredients of gourmet baking, especially in the form of chestnut purée used for tarts, cakes and desserts. Then there is the candied chestnut, the French *marron glacee* which the Turks enjoy as *kestane şekeri*. These are plump, syrup-coated delicacies with a heavenly taste, traditionally specific to the Bursa region on the southern shore of the Marmara Sea, but today commercially prepared in Istanbul and other major cities. When winter is upon the city, the familiar and long-awaited signs appear on the windows of distinguished patisseries: "Seasonal candied chestnuts have arrived!"

Candied Chestnuts *Kestane Sekeri* [3]

Ingredients

Chestnuts	500 g, shelled
Granulated sugar	350 g
Vanilla powder	2 tsp

Method

- Place the shelled chestnuts in a pot with enough water to cover and boil on low heat until they are tender and the inner skins can be easily removed.
- Place the sugar in a large pot and fill with water to cover just above the sugar, about 1.5 cm. Wait for the sugar to dissolve; do not stir. When the sugar melts, add the chestnuts and cook on low heat for 2 hours. Do not boil. Remove from the heat and let stand for 24 hours. Cook again on low heat until all the remaining syrup is absorbed. Arrange the chestnuts individually on a dish and sprinkle with vanilla powder. It is ready for serving.

Marble Cake with Chestnuts *Kestaneli Mozaik Pasta*
(Serves 8–10)

Ingredients

Petit beurre or any other plain tea biscuits	300 g
Chestnuts	750 g
Margarine	125 g
Eggs	2
Milk	120 ml
Icing (confectioners') sugar	3 Tbsp
Cocoa powder	3 Tbsp

Method

- Break the biscuits into a large bowl with your fingers; the pieces will be irregular in shape and size.
- Slit the chestnuts and put them into a pot. Cover with water. When the water comes to the boil, cook for 5 minutes; do not overcook. Drain the water, rinse the chestnuts with cold water and peel them. This is the most time consuming and difficult part of this recipe but it is worth the effort. Transfer the chestnuts into the bowl with the biscuits.
- Melt the margarine over low heat in a small pan and pour over the biscuits and chestnuts.
- In a separate bowl, mix the eggs well, add the milk and pour this liquid mixture to the bowl. Sprinkle the icing sugar and the cocoa powder over the mixture as well and start mixing with a spatula. Mix well until all the dry ingredients are moistened. It may look dry in the beginning but as you continue, all the biscuits and chestnuts will be coated. Since there is no cooking, it is important to mix all the ingredients thoroughly.
- Pour this mixture into a non-stick mould. Keep in the refrigerator for at least 2 hours and then turn onto the serving plate and slice individual servings. Serve with chocolate sauce or vanilla ice cream or simply sprinkle icing sugar on top.

local bananas, Anamur

BANANAS *Muz*

Bananas probably first grew in Southeast Asia and were then
brought from India to the Middle East and then to Africa
in the early Islamic period. Spanish and Portuguese colonists
took bananas across the Atlantic from Africa to the Americas,
also bringing along the African name, *"banana"*, apparently
a word from one of the languages of the Congo area. It has been
speculated that the name was ultimately derived from Arabic
"banana", meaning "finger" or "toe," as also echoed in the English
term, "hand," for a bunch of bananas.[1] There is a Hindu legend
in which the banana was the fruit forbidden to Adam and Eve
in the terrestrial paradise. After consuming the fruit, they
covered their nakedness with banana leaves. This perhaps
explains the names "Adam's fig tree" and "Paradise banana",
which the Indians have given to two species of the banana tree

The banana is very rich in nutrition. It provides a sufficient
quantity of all the mineral salts necessary for the body's daily
maintenance. It is rich in starch which is transformed into
energising sugar when the fruit is fully ripe and is also rich
in vitamins A, B, B1, B2, B12, D and E.

In Turkey, bananas grow along the Mediterranean coast,
especially in the stretch between Mersin and Anamur where
the steep hills are terraced for the miniature plantations.
Smaller but much sweeter than the recently imported varieties
from California and South America, they have a distinct and
very pleasant fragrance. This domestic variety appears in
Turkish streets only in winter and since the 1980s, it has been
losing out to the imported bananas that have conquered
a mass-market for year-round consumption.

Banana Bread *Muzlu Kek*
(Makes 1 loaf)

Ingredients

Plain (all-purpose) flour	200 g
Ground cinnamon	1 tsp
Baking powder	1 tsp
Bicarbonate of soda	1 tsp
Salt	$^{1}/_{2}$ tsp
Granulated sugar	200 g
Eggs	3
Vegetable oil	150 ml
Ripe bananas	3
Walnuts	120 g, chopped

Method

- Sift the flour, ground cinnamon, baking powder, bicarbonate of soda and salt together. Set aside.
- Combine the sugar and eggs in a mixer, then add the oil. Peel and purée the bananas and add to the mixer. Add the dry ingredients and mix just enough to incorporate. Do not over mix. Add the chopped walnuts and stir with a spatula. Pour onto a greased and floured loaf tin.
- Preheat the oven to 170°C and bake for 30 minutes. Check that the bread is done by inserting a skewer and pulling it out. If it comes out clean, the bread is done. If not, bake for a further 5–10 minutes.

Banana Shake *Muzlu Süt*

Nothing can be more delicious or nutritious than a quick banana shake in the morning when you do not have the time or the habit for breakfast. You can substitute honey with maple syrup for a change of flavour.

(Serves 1)

Ingredients

Milk	250 ml
Banana	1
Honey	1 Tbsp
Ground cinnamon	$\frac{1}{2}$ tsp
Ground ginger	$\frac{1}{2}$ tsp

Method

- Pour the milk into a blender. Add the banana, honey, cinnamon and ginger. Blend.

FISH *Balık*

From the early hours of the morning, fishing boats start coming into Istanbul's wholesale fish market located in Yenikapı on the southern shore of the historical peninsula. Retailers, purchasers for restaurants and many others make a busy, noisy crowd. It is the first week of winter and the market is already overflowing with the catch of *hamsi*. Crates of the fish are piled on top of each other. With such abundance, they are sold not by the kilogram but by the crate. In another part of the market, turbots are heaped on the ground. Swordfish, sea bass, bonito, mussels and prawns (shrimps) of different sizes also abound, together with blue fin *(istavrit)*, some of them arriving from as far as Tuzla on the Asian side of the Marmara Sea. The fish are covered with crushed ice; their eyes are shiny (an unfailing mark of freshness) and their scaled bodies glow with shades of pink and purple in the early morning light.

Working from their boats that are transformed into kitchenettes, the fish-and-bread sellers of Eminönü feed both the people and the seagulls of Istanbul throughout the year with different varieties of fish. At the point where the legendary Golden Horn meets the Marmara Sea, in front of the Valide Sultan Mosque *(Yeni Cami)* and the Spice Bazaar, and just next to the imperial grounds of the Topkapı Palace where Ottoman sultans reigned for centuries, the smell and smoke of frying fish mixes with the shrill cries of the seagulls, capturing the bystanders in what can best be described as a commotion and a sensory feast at the same time. In many other parts along Istanbul's shore, such kitchenette-boats line up side-by-side from the wee hours of the morning, waiting for their first customers. A piece of fried fish sandwiched in a half or quarter loaf of fresh bread makes a tasty and affordable meal for Istanbul's crowds throughout the day. After sunset, as the evening descends on the sea, it is possible to see small groups of men arranging a makeshift table next to these boats, to eat their fish-and-bread, accompanied with a small glass of *rakı* (a popular anisette drink with an alcohol content of 45 per cent).

From top Early morning in Istanbul's wholesale fish market; Swordfish catch

Raw fish is not a very common item in Turkish culinary culture, perhaps with the sole exception of salted bonito *(lakerda). Lakerda* is a special delicacy of Turkish cuisine, a kind of "Turkish sushi" and an extremely popular appetiser *(meze)* that can be found in most fish restaurants. The presentation of *lakerda* is very simple and for a good reason: a well-prepared *lakerda* offers an aesthetically pleasing texture by itself, often served with slices of red onions or a few pieces of spring onions (scallions). To complete to perfection the culinary experience of eating *lakerda*, one must also have some feta cheese, slices of melon, if in season, a simple salad and of course, a glass of *rakı*!

Salted Bonito *Lakerda*

An Istanbul fisherman, Nazmi Yeşil, demonstrates the intricacies of making *lakerda. Lakerda* is made from either *palamut* or *torik*, both of them varieties of the bonito family. *Torik*, the more fatty fish of the two, is the preferred variety. The *lakerda* preparation season extends from September to November and discerning customers often give their orders long before that, indicating their preference for either *palamut* or *torik*. As for the procedure: first the fish is cut along its belly and cleaned thoroughly, its head and fins discarded. It is then sliced into pieces 6–7 cm thick. Pushing a thin needle back and forth through the centre of each slice, Nazmi Yeşil carefully cleans the marrow and any accumulated blood, explaining that this is the most important step in *lakerda*-making to prevent undesirable smells.

The clean pieces of fish are covered with fresh water and kept in the refrigerator for 24 hours. They are then removed from the water, dried and completely covered with table salt. It takes about two weeks in the refrigerator for salted *torik* to be ready and about 5–6 days for salted *palamut*. The pieces of fish are then rinsed, portioned and kept in olive oil in jars or cans.

Fish with *Tahin Helvası*

The most typical and desirable ending for any fish meal would be a few thin slabs of a popular sesame paste dessert *(tahin helvası)* that comes in two varieties: plain or with pistachios. Although *helva* is a generic name for the numerous varieties of this dessert

mentioned in Ottoman treatises and archival records,[5] it is often used to designate *tahin helvası*, testifying to the latter's popularity as "the *helva* par excellence". The close association between fish and *helva* (the pervasive belief that the two go together very well, making a healthy combination) is not simply a product of popular imagination, but goes back to Ottoman history. The prominent 17th century chronicler/traveller, Evliya Çelebi, writes that before the Baghdad campaign of Sultan Murat IV, an elaborate parade was organised with representatives of different guilds, including cooks, sherbet makers and other culinary artists showing off their skills in front of the sultan. During this parade, a dispute broke out between the *helva* makers and fish cooks regarding which group would parade first. The *helva* makers referred to literary pieces and gave Koranic evidence to argue that fish is not good for health, causing "light headedness" and that *helva* was Prophet Mohammed's favoured recommendation for the faithful, thus winning the contest against the fish cooks.[6] Although Evliya Çelebi does not make the deduction, it is most likely that the fish-*helva* combination originated from this belief, to neutralise the effects of fish with a piece of *helva* at the end.

Fish seller, late 19th century (Istanbul Metropolitan Municipality, Atatürk Library)

From top left Preparation of *lakerda*; Bottled *lakerda*; A plate of *lakerda*

Grilled Sardines in Vine Leaves *Asma Yapragında Sardalya*
(Serves 4)

Ingredients

Vine leaves	500 g, fresh or preserved
Sardines	1 kg
Extra virgin olive oil	2 Tbsp
Freshly ground black pepper	to taste
Salt	to taste
Lemons	2, sliced in rounds

Method

- If using vine leaves preserved in brine, soak them in warm water and drain for a couple of times. If using fresh leaves, keep them in hot water for a short time depending on the tenderness of the leaves.
- Gut the sardines and discard the heads, fillet the fish.
- Nip off the stalks of the vine leaves and arrange them on the counter, vein sides up. Brush them with olive oil, sprinkle black pepper and salt if necessary. Place sardines on the leaves and wrap them loosely as with a package.
- Grill the lemon slices until there are grill marks on both sides. Place them over a bed of salad on the serving plate.
- Grill the sardines, about 3 minutes each side, until there are grill marks, flipping gently. Serve them over the grilled lemon slices. Alternatively, you can add a layer of grilled red bell peppers over the sardines.

Sea Bass with Sautéed Mushrooms and Courgettes *Sote Mantar ve Kabaklı Levrek*
(Serves 4)

Ingredients

Red bell peppers	2
Olive oil	2 Tbsp
Onion	1, peeled, quartered and thinly sliced
Button mushrooms	100 g, coarsely chopped
Shiitake mushrooms	100 g, sliced lengthwise
Lemon juice	extracted from ¹/₂ lemon
Salt	to taste
Freshly ground black pepper	to taste
Courgettes (zucchinis)	2, cut into 1 cm cubes
Granulated sugar	1 Tbsp
Corn flour (cornstarch)	60 g
Sea bass	1, large, cleaned and cut into 4 fillets
Cooking oil for frying	

Basil Sauce

Basil	1 bunch
Garlic	1 clove, peeled and chopped
Salt and ground black pepper	
Lemon juice	extracted from ¹/₂ lemon
Extra virgin olive oil	60 ml

Garnish

Basil	a few sprigs

Method

- First prepare the basil sauce. Pick the best leaves of the basil and set aside. Blanch the rest in boiling water for 1 minute and immerse in ice-cold water. Drain and squeeze well. Transfer to a blender; add the garlic, salt, pepper and lemon juice and blend. Add the olive oil in a thin stream while blending. Set aside.
- Fry the reserved basil leaves for a few minutes in oil over low heat until translucent. Set aside.
- Wash the bell peppers and put them over open heat on the stove, flipping them over as they blacken. When ready, put in a bowl and cover with cling film for 5 minutes. This will make them easier to peel. Peel then slice them into lengths about 1-cm thick.
- Heat the olive oil on medium heat and cook the onions, mushrooms, lemon juice, salt and pepper. When the mushrooms are about to be ready, add the strips of bell pepper and mix generously. Remove from heat and keep aside, covered.
- In the same pan, cook the courgettes and sprinkle the sugar on top together with some salt and pepper. Cook for 7–8 minutes until tender, stirring occasionally. When ready, remove from the heat.
- Mix the corn flour and some salt and pepper. Coat the fish fillets well in this mixture and fry them in well-heated oil, about 2 minutes each side, until crisp and golden brown outside, but still juicy inside.
- Decorate the serving plate with a circle of basil. Using ring moulds, fill with sautéed mushrooms, then with sautéed courgettes, patting gently until the mould is completely full. Very carefully remove the mould and place a fish fillet on top.
- Sprinkle basil sauce around and garnish with fried basil leaves.

Baked Salmon on Spinach Purée
Ispanak Püresi Üzerinde Somon
(Serves 4)

Ingredients

Norwegian salmon	4 slices
Balsamic vinegar	4 Tbsp
Honey	2 Tbsp
Grated ginger	1 tsp
Salt and ground black pepper	
Spinach	750 g, roots and thick stems removed
Butter	2 Tbsp
Plain (all-purpose) flour	2 Tbsp
Heavy cream	100 ml
Milk	200 ml
Ground nutmeg	$^1\!/_2$ tsp

Method

- Place the salmon slices in an oven dish. Set aside. In a bowl, mix well the balsamic vinegar, honey, grated ginger, salt and pepper. Spread the mixture on the salmon with a pastry brush or with your fingers. Cover and refrigerate for an hour.
- Meanwhile, prepare the purée. Wash the spinach well and steam for couple of minutes until tender. Remove from the steamer and let it rest in a colander. Squeeze of excess water then process in a blender.
- In a pot, melt the butter, add the flour and mix well with a wooden spoon until it turns golden brown. Add the cream and the milk and keep stirring with a whisk to avoid lumps. The mixture should have a very thick consistency. Add the salt, pepper and the nutmeg and then add the puréed spinach and continue to stir with the wooden spoon. Cook for 2 minutes, remove from the heat and adjust seasoning.
- Heat the oven to 175°C. Turn the salmon slices over and broil for 8–10 minutes, depending on the thickness of the slices. Do not overcook or it will be dry.
- Spoon some spinach purée on a serving plate and arrange a salmon slice on top of it. Serve immediately.

Swordfish with Spinach Mousse
Ispanak Mus ile Kılıç Balığı
(Serves 4)

Ingredients

Swordfish	4 slices, each about 1-cm thick, bone and skin removed
Salt and ground black pepper	
Extra virgin olive oil	2 Tbsp
Fennel bulbs	2, sliced
Garlic	7–8 cloves, peeled
Tomatoes	400 g, chopped
Lemon	1, sliced
Capers	2 Tbsp
Bay leaves	
Oregano	

Spinach Mousse

Spinach	750 g, stems removed
Eggs	2
Salt and ground white pepper	
Heavy cream	200 ml
Ground nutmeg	a pinch

Method

- Preheat the oven to 170°C.
- Prepare the spinach mousse. Steam the spinach for 2 minutes until tender but still firm and green. Transfer to a colander. Squeeze the spinach to get rid of the excess of water and transfer to a blender. Add the eggs, salt, pepper and heavy cream, then pulse the blender until well-mixed. (Mixing at high speed without pulsing will result in foam.) Pour the mixture into buttered ramekins and bake for 40 minutes in a water bath until set. When ready, remove the water and let it cool in the oven. (While the mousse is in the oven, cut the top of garlic stems and brush with a few drops of olive oil. Wrap in aluminium foil and bake for 15–20 minutes to accompany the fish.)
- With the help of a knife, turn the mousse onto serving plates.
- Prepare the fish. Season both sides with salt and pepper and cook in a non-stick pan for about 2 minutes each side, before removing to the serving plate.
- Heat the olive oil in the same pan. First add the sliced fennel with the garlic cloves and cook until browned. Then add the tomatoes, lemon slices, capers, bay leaves and oregano. Cook for a few more minutes before pouring over the fish to serve.

Stuffed mussels, Haydarpaşa Railway Station, Istanbul

Mussels for sale, fish market, Ayvalık

MUSSELS *Midye*

Although clams, oysters and other shellfish are uncommon
in Turkey, mussels enjoy wide popularity as *mezes*. There is no
chowder in Turkish cuisine and mussels are commonly eaten
in two ways: as fried mussels *(midye tava)* or stuffed mussels
(midye dolma), an unusual dish in which a spicy rice with
currants and pine nuts is prepared separately and then stuffed
into the mussel shells and cooked again with the mussels.

As the seas are getting increasingly more polluted,
it is getting harder to guarantee the safety of eating mussels.
So far, however, most people sipping their beers or *rakı*
with mussel *mezes* seem unconcerned.

Fried *Hamsi* on Mashed Peas and Potatoes
Patates ve Bezelye Püreli Hamsi Tava
(Serves 4)

Ingredients

Hamsi (fresh anchovies)	750 g
Frozen peas	300 g
Butter	1 Tbsp
Onion	1, peeled and coarsely chopped
Plain (all-purpose) flour	3 Tbsp
Heavy cream	200 ml
Potatoes	3, peeled
Egg yolk	1
Salt and ground white pepper	
Cooking oil for frying	
Lumpfish caviar	4 tsp

Method

- Gut the *hamsi* and remove the heads. Remove the bone as well and butterfly them. Wash well, drain and pat dry. Set aside.
- Steam the peas until soft. Dip into ice-cold water for some seconds to retain their colour. In a pan, melt the butter and add the onion. Sweat for couple of minutes and sprinkle in 1 Tbsp flour. Mix with a wooden spoon to avoid lumps. Add half of the cream and continue mixing until it bubbles and comes to a thick consistency. Then add the peas and mash with the back of the spoon as you continue to cook over low heat for 2 minutes. Remove from heat and set aside.
- Boil the potatoes until soft. Mash with the back of a spoon, add the remaining cream, egg yolk, some salt and pepper, and mix well. Set aside.
- Put the remaining flour on a plate, sprinkle some salt over and mix well. Place the *hamsi* over the flour and coat both sides. Shake off excess flour. Fry in a pan of oil over high heat until golden brown. Transfer to a plate and drain on paper towels.
- To serve, place a ring mould in the middle of the plate. Spoon some of the mashed peas into the ring and gently press down with the spoon. Top with the potato mash and remove the mould. Arrange the *hamsi* over the mash and top with caviar.

Fried Mussels *Midye Tava*
(Serves 4)

Ingredients

Mussels	400 g, shelled and cleaned
Plain (all-purpose) flour	4 Tbsp
Salt	a pinch
Baking soda	1 Tbsp
Water	1 litre
Cooking oil for frying	

Method

- Arrange the mussels on skewers. Mix the flour and salt well. Roll the skewered mussels on the flour and coat well.
- Stir the baking soda into the water and dip the skewered mussels in. Heat the cooking oil over high heat and fry the mussels. Serve warm with tartar sauce.

Winter vegetables, Izmir

Salad greens, Balat, Istanbul

SALAD GREENS

"A main course without a salad is like a chinchilla whose fur has fallen off," remarks Murat Belge in his book about culinary cultures of the world, also lamenting that the art of preparing a salad is not always fully appreciated.[7] Like most Mediterranean countries, Turkey is blessed with an abundance of ingredients for salads, which are typically eaten with the meal rather than before (as in Anglo-Saxon cultures) or after (as the French do). The rich variety of salad greens that embellish street carts in the spring include lettuces of different kinds: the curlier *kıvırcık* and the straight-leaved romaine lettuce *(marul)*, the exquisite bitter rocket that is a regional favorite of gourmet salads in Turkey, Greece and Italy, bunches of *tere*, an even more bitter green that goes particularly well with the meat dishes of southeastern Turkey, fresh basil, fresh dill and of course the versatile fresh parsley which is used to flavour and/or garnish almost any dish. (According to Murat Belge, the parsley is overused, often inappropriately, giving rise to the expression: *herşeye maydonoz olmak* ("being the parsley in everything"), used in common parlance for overzealous people who want to be involved in matters that do not concern them.) Other salad 'greens' like fraise, endives, radicchio and watercress are harder to find in Turkey, perhaps except in gourmet grocery stores in Istanbul and Ankara. Thoroughly washed and properly dried greens with a simple dressing of olive oil, lemon and vinegar always make an indispensable and appetising companion to fish dishes.

WINTER VEGETABLES

Throughout the winter, fresh produce markets and street carts overflow with a rich array of vegetables—the indispensable ingredients of hearty home cooking. Preserved in the earth and therefore highly resistant to frost and cold, root vegetables like onions, leeks, potatoes, carrots and celery are basic staple foods used in stews and soups. Leeks *(pırasa)* and celery *(kereviz)* make exquisite dishes when cooked in olive oil, typically served as appetisers or as a digestive course after the main dish. Of the leaf vegetables, spinach, cabbage and cauliflower are also widely popular in Turkey, used for countless dishes including such traditionally famous 'Turkish' items like spinach pastries *(ıspanaklı börek)* and stuffed cabbage leaves *(lahana dolması)*. People widely share the pervasive (and not necessarily accurate) popular belief about spinach being a very rich source of iron— a belief the origin of which cultural historian Murat Belge traces to a misprint in one encyclopedic source giving the mineral content of various vegetables.[8] Less contentious are the benefits of carrots for the eyes and as a rich source of vitamin C. A simple bowl of grated carrots with a drizzle of lemon juice and olive oil makes a popular winter salad in most households. But that is not all! Most snack kiosks *(büfe)* in busy public spaces of the city offer freshly squeezed carrot juice in the winter. Finally, an unusual sweet consisting of carrot and walnut squares *(cezerye*, originally a specialty of the Mersin region in the south) can be found in specialty sweet shops everywhere, demonstrating the range of the culinary possibilities of this common vegetable.

Honey and Mustard Salad Dressing *Bal ve Hardallı Salata Sosu*
(Makes about 250 ml)

Ingredients

Garlic	3 cloves, peeled
Mustard	1 Tbsp
Honey	2 Tbsp
Lemon juice	extracted from 1 lemon
Salt and ground black pepper	
Ground ginger	½ tsp
Balsamic vinegar or pomegranate vinegar	60 ml
Extra virgin olive oil	180 ml

Method

- Mash the garlic through a garlic press. Put into a jar or a container with a lid.
- Add the mustard, honey, lemon juice, salt, pepper and ginger and mix well with a spoon. Add the balsamic or pomegranate vinegar and close the lid. Shake well. Finally add the olive oil and shake vigorously.
- Keep the dressing at room temperature. It will keep for days. Shake well before each use.

Carrot Dessert *Havuç Tatlısı*
(Serves 4)

Ingredients

Carrot	750 g, peeled and grated
Granulated sugar	110 g
Ground cinnamon	1 tsp
Ground nutmeg	1 tsp
Walnuts	200 g, chopped + more for topping
Heavy cream	300 ml
Bitter chocolate	200 g, broken in pieces
Chocolate crispies (with cocoa powder)	40 g

Method

- In a shallow pan, cook the grated carrots with the sugar, cinnamon and nutmeg until tender or about 30 minutes on low heat. Add the walnuts and remove from the heat.
- In a bowl, whisk the heavy cream until stiff. Divide into two bowls. Add the chocolate crispies into one of the bowls and mix well.
- Put a deep pan over heat with some water and bring to the boil. Place a bowl over the pan, making sure that the base does not touch the water. Melt the chocolate in this bowl then add the plain whipped heavy cream, stirring constantly.
- First place a layer of the carrot mix into serving bowls. Press down with the back of a spoon. Add some of the whipped heavy cream with the chocolate crispies and finally the chocolate cream. Repeat the layering. Decorate with whole and ground walnuts.

Onion and potato truck, Istanbul

ONIONS AND POTATOES

Soğan ve Patates

Even in the most remote neighbourhoods of Istanbul, it is not uncommon to see a small truck pass by residential streets, its driver shouting through loudspeakers mounted on top of the truck, *"Patates var, soğan var!"* ("Potatoes are here, onions are here!") Although potatoes are popular in Turkey, this predominantly bread-eating country is not associated with potatoes the way Germany or Ireland are. Culinary historians talk about initial prejudices against the potato in grain-growing regions of Europe—that potatoes are lowly vegetables fit only for pigs—after they were brought from the Americas and introduced in the European diet roughly between the 16th and 18th centuries.[9] Murat Belge writes that it was not until the Napoleonic Wars that potato became the basic staple of European peasantry, as being a root vegetable hidden deep in the ground, potatoes were able to survive these wars when all other grains and entire fields were destroyed.[10] In Turkey, although potatoes and various members of the onion family (onions, spring onions (scallions), leeks and shallots) are grown in almost every part of the country, the potatoes and red onions of the Adapazarı region in the northwest are particularly famous for their taste and texture, sold in large sacks lined along the roads. As a result, many street sellers of Istanbul bring their potatoes and onions from Adapazarı.

There is ample evidence that potato dishes were abundant in imperial Ottoman cuisine and fancier versions of potato purées, fries and crockets adorn gourmet dishes in many restaurants today. Nonetheless, this fairly cheap and winter resistant root vegetable still maintains a general reputation for being the basic staple of the poor, along with its companion, the onion, slices of which garnish grilled meatballs or other kebabs sold in the streets. Due to its rich carbohydrate content, the figure-conscious try to avoid the potato but do not always succeed, becoming *patates gibi şişman* ("fat as a potato"), a common expression in the Turkish language.

Lamb Chops with Caramelised Onions and Sautéed Potatoes
Karamelize Soğan ve Sote Patatesli Kuzu Pirzola
(Serves 4)

Ingredients

Lamb chops	12
Salt and ground black pepper	
Oregano	

Caramelised Onions

Butter	1 Tbsp
Onions	4, large, peeled and cut thinly in rings
Red wine	125 ml

Sautéed Potatoes

Potatoes	4
Vegetable oil	
Garlic	2 cloves, peeled and thinly sliced
Rosemary	1 sprig, chopped

Method

- Prepare the caramelised onions. Heat the butter in a pan and add the onions. Let them cook over low heat for 1 hour, stirring occasionally. At the end of the hour, they should have a light caramel colour, retaining some juice. Then, add the red wine and cook for 30 minutes more with the lid closed over low heat.
- Prepare the potatoes. Wash well and submerge in a pot of water. Add some salt and bring to the boil. Let it simmer until the potatoes are tender. Check with the tip of a knife and drain. Peel the potatoes and cut into 0.5-cm cubes.
- In a pan, add some vegetable oil then add the garlic and sauté for a few seconds. Add the potatoes, some salt and pepper and the rosemary. Sauté over high heat for 1–2 minutes until the sides of the potatoes are golden brown. Remove from heat and set aside.
- Heat a grill until very hot, then put in a few drops of vegetable oil. Season the lamb chops with salt and pepper and some oregano and place over the grill. Sear both sides over high heat and grill according to taste.
- To serve, place a spoonful of caramelised onions on a serving plate and arrange the lamb chops around it. Accompany with sautéed potatoes on the side.

Lamb Shanks with Potatoes, Pearl Onions and Fava Beans
Patates, Soğan ve İç Baklalı Kuzu Incik
(Serves 4)

Ingredients

Butter	2 Tbsp
Olive oil	3 Tbsp
Lamb shanks	4
Salt and ground black pepper	
Garlic	6 cloves, peeled and roughly chopped
Red wine	500 ml
Bay leaves	4
Pearl onions	16, peeled
Sugar	1 Tbsp
Potatoes	4, peeled and cut into 3-mm slices
Fava beans	250 g
Dill	1 bunch, coarsely chopped
Cooking oil for frying	
Chilli flakes	

Method

- Heat 1 Tbsp butter and 1 Tbsp olive oil in a pan until very hot.
- Season the lamb shanks with salt and pepper and place in the pan. Sear all sides of the shanks over high heat. Remove the shanks and discard the excess oil. Put in the garlic and return the shanks to the pan. Pour the wine over them. Add the bay leaves and when the liquid comes to the boil, reduce the heat and close the lid. Cook simmering until tender, for about 45 minutes.
- Meanwhile prepare the onions. Place the pearl onions in a pot filled with water halfway to the height of the onions. Add the remaining butter and the sugar, a pinch of salt and bring to the boil. Let the onion cook, shaking the pot from time to time. When all the water is gone, continue shaking the pan and let the onions caramelise for a short time. Then add 3–4 Tbsp of water and shake until all is evaporated. Watch carefully, otherwise you may easily burn the onions and the pot. When ready, set aside.
- Heat the oil and fry the potatoes. Transfer to a plate lined with paper towels to drain. Lightly salt them and set aside.
- Steam the fava beans for 5 minutes until tender. Dip into a bowl of iced water to retain their colour.
- Put the remaining olive oil in another pan and cook the fava beans for a few minutes. Chop the dill coarsely and add to the fava beans just before you remove the pan from the heat.
- Before serving, mix the potatoes, pearl onions and the fava beans in a deep bowl and toss well. Put a generous amount on a serving plate. Wrap the tip of the lamb shank with aluminium foil and place the shank over the vegetables. Sprinkle chilli flakes on top.

PICKLES *Turşu*

This traditional method of preserving vegetables continues to be prominent in Turkish cuisine, although home pickling is an increasingly rare ritual nowadays, giving way to commercially prepared pickles. Cucumbers, tomatoes, chillies, cabbage, green beans, carrots and aubergines (eggplants) are the most common pickling items. After being washed and cut as necessary, they are stuffed into large jars with garlic cloves, lemon salt, water and vinegar and left there until they are "done". Although pickles are eaten in almost every season, the absence of fresh summer vegetables makes pickles even more desirable in winter. Jars of colourful pickles have enormous aesthetic appeal as well, as can be observed in the displays of street carts or in traditional restaurants like Hacı Abdullah in Istanbul where large pickle jars constitute some of the interior decoration.

Different metaphorical and idiomatic references to pickles exist in the Turkish language, testifying to the widely shared knowledge of this process within the culture. Pickling *(turşu kurmak)* is a common expression designating the act of storing something for a long period of time without using it. A familiar expression, *turşum çıktı* ("turning into a pickle") designates a state of utmost physical exhaustion and loss of energy.

Clockwise from top left Pickle cart, Eminönü, Istanbul; Hot chilli pickles, Izmir; Assorted pickles in jars, Adana

Burma dessert, Ankara

Burma dessert, better known as *kerhane tatlısı*, Karaköy, Istanbul

***BURMA* DESSERT** *Burma Tatlısı*

"*Burma*" (literally "twisted") is a very common and popular street dessert that one can come across in different Turkish cities. The seller in Ankara has taken over this tradition from his father, continuing the family business. He prepares the dessert at home, mixing four different types of flour and yeast into a soft dough. Squeezing the dough through a fluted tip, he fries rings of dough in sunflower oil and dips them in a simple syrup of sugar and water. He says that this light dessert, prepared fresh, sells very well and on a typical day, he returns home with none left on his tray. With one piece selling for about US$0.35, the cheapness of the *burma* dessert undoubtedly contributes to its popularity. However, like most street sellers of Turkey, he complains about the municipality that is increasingly less tolerant of street foods, frequently confiscating carts and imposing substantial fines. When summer comes, he switches to making and selling ice cream.

The same dessert can take different names in different cities and localities. In a less reputable district of Istanbul famous for its brothels, *burma* dessert is known as *kerhane tatlısı*, literally "brothel dessert" promising a sweet ending to various commercial exchanges that take place in the area at night.

Calling into the night, *boza* seller, Nişantaşı, Istanbul

Boza with cinnamon

BOZA

Boza is a thick, fermented drink made from millet, wheat, rice, corn and oats. Its origins can be traced to Central Asia and it is believed to have spread to Anatolia, Bulgaria, Romania and the Balkans. The most famous *boza* manufacturers of Istanbul during the Ottoman Empire were Armenians, and more than 300 *boza* stores are known to have existed in 17th century Istanbul. During the reign of Murad IV, the alcohol ban enforced in the city was extended to *boza*, although its alcohol content is only about one per cent (with the exception of some Caucasian versions that can go up to six per cent). In that period, *boza* was known to have gone 'underground' and the practice of mixing it with opium tainted its name further. It was only after the lifting of the ban that normal *boza* production resumed, establishing it as a popular and respectable drink. Today in Turkey, *boza* is immediately associated with two famous manufacturers, Vefa Bozası in Istanbul and Akman Bozası in Ankara, to the extent that *boza* sellers in Istanbul advertise their product as "Vefa Bozasi" even when they have no link to the establishment that only sells its *boza* in a few known stores. (The history of Vefa Bozasi goes back about 125 years when two brothers from Yugoslavia opened a store in the Vefa district of Istanbul.)

The taste of *boza* can display significant variations from the sweet to the slightly bitter or sour. Although the techniques and tools of production have changed over the centuries, these tastes have remained constant. In the past, *boza* was prepared in huge copper cauldrons and manually stirred with large wooden spoons. Now production is largely mechanised. After it is thoroughly boiled and filtered, sugar is added and the fermentation process begins. The preparation of *boza* takes about 24 hours from start to finish, and its shelf life is about a week after which it starts to go sour. It is perceived as a popular remedy for stomach and intestinal problems and is strongly recommended for pregnant women and nursing mothers.

Boza sellers are a characteristic feature of cold winter nights in Turkey, carrying their plastic containers and shouting into the night to announce their arrival. (Some also sell roasted chickpeas *(leblebi)* as an accompaniment—it is widely believed that since *boza* is a fermented drink, the chickpeas prevent any potential discomfort to sensitive stomachs.) Although *boza* is popularly sold throughout the year elsewhere, such as Bulgaria, the Turks seem to believe that it can be too heavy in the summer, just as they associate ice cream exclusively with summer months.

Albanian *boza* seller, 17th century (*Kıyafetname* manuscript, Berlin Kunstbibliothek; from the collection of Galeri Alfa)

A cup of *sahlep*, sprinkled with cinnamon and ginger

SAHLEP

This other popular drink of cold winter months is made from the *sahlep* plant, a kind of wild orchid (the Orchis) with a straight, red stem, purple flowers and potato-like roots. Typically, the Orchis has two of these roots working in tandem, one storing nutrients for the following season while the other feeds the plant. Every year, the latter is used to produce the *sahlep* while the former is buried in the ground for the following year. In traditional *sahlep* preparation, the roots are cleaned, then boiled and dried in the sun. They are then ground into a fine powder. *Sahlep* used to be a reputed herbal remedy. The famous London astrologer/physician Nicholas Culpeper refers to *sahlep* in his *Complete Herbal*.[11] About Orchis (Satyrium) he says, "*Sahlep* is a preparation of the roots, of which there are many species according to the soil they grow in...*Sahlep* contains the greatest quantity of nourishment in the smallest bulk and will support the system in privation and during famine, it is good for those who travel long distances and are compelled to endure exposure without food." He also mentions that the plant can "provoke lust".

The most common way to make *sahlep* is by mixing a teaspoonful of it with milk, sugar to taste and half a teaspoonful of starch. It should be stirred constantly while heating until it comes to the boil. It is usually served sprinkled with cinnamon and ginger on top. Consumed especially in winter, *sahlep* is known to be an effective remedy for colds, stomach disturbances and asthma-like breathing difficulties.

Brass *sahlep* fountains, Taksim Square, Istanbul

SPRING

Spring flowers of many colours and fragrances—
daffodils, tulips, lilies and a little later, roses—line up
along the streets competing with the colours, textures
and smells of fresh fruits and vegetables.

Once the first crocuses and narcissus emerge from the melting snow and bunches of them appear for sale in the streets, one knows that winter is almost over. When the strawberries *(çilek)* arrive in baskets, the end of another winter becomes official. Spring flowers of many colours and fragrances—daffodils, tulips, lilies and a little later, roses— line up along the streets competing with the colours, textures and smells of fresh fruits and vegetables. The first artichokes, cucumbers and strawberries come from the gardens of the Mediterranean and Aegean coasts, to be soon replaced by local produce from around Istanbul and the Marmara region. By mid April, a visible revival of street life and commerce can be observed in most Turkish cities, especially in Istanbul where the city's more than 10 million inhabitants begin carrying their everyday life outdoors. As they run their errands, they stop for a short lunch break with gyro *(döner)*, grilled meatballs *(köftes)* and a salted yoghurt drink *(ayran)*, national fast-food of Turkish people.

In the southeast, where spring starts much earlier, April, May and June are almost as warm as summer but not as uncomfortable yet. Many of the local specialties can best be enjoyed in these months in the streets of Gaziantep, Urfa, Adana and Antakya, from refreshing fruit coolers to varieties of milk puddings and local *baklavas*. For example, in cosmopolitan Antakya, Turkey's southernmost city with a rich historical heritage and a world-famous museum of Roman mosaics, the makers/sellers of *künefe*, a shredded wheat dessert, line up along the river Orontes and the old bazaar awakens to each new day with the busy routine of *kadayıf* (shredded wheat) makers, cheese merchants and small shops serving hummus and fava bean spreads. Men flock into the popular Hidro Restaurant where one can taste the best *zahter* salad—a delicious local specialty made with fresh *zahter* (resembling rosemary in shape but tasting like oregano), tomatoes, onions and pomegranate vinegar. Women chat in front of brick ovens exposed to the street, waiting for the pepper pita breads *(biberli pide)* and meat and bulgur patties *(içli köfte)* another local delicacy of the southeast, made of fine bulgur and ground beef, known as *oruk* in that part of Turkey, to be ready. It is as if, the five senses blunted by the dreariness of the winter, finally come alive when street foods appear everywhere in the spring.

Opposite, clockwise from top Local cheeses, Adana; Sack of fresh *zahter*, Antakya; Liver kebabs, Gaziantep

ARTICHOKES *Enginar*

Sadık, who sells his artichokes in the wealthy neighbourhood of Teşvikiye in Istanbul, has migrated from the eastern Anatolian town of Malatya. In early spring, he buys the artichokes from his uncle's farm in Izmir on the western coast of Turkey. These artichokes, among the first ones to ripen, are slightly smaller and known as *sakız enginar*, probably in reference to the pure whiteness of their insides. As Sadık explains, a few weeks into the spring, the artichokes of Bursa (to the south of Istanbul) and its surroundings begin to ripen and the entire season lasts about three months at the most. According to Sadık, the last artichokes of the season are often inferior in taste and are more fibrous.

Preparing the artichokes is an art in itself. Sadık cuts the stems carefully and removes the lower leaves first. Then, holding the artichoke firmly in his left hand, he uses his right hand to peel and carve it with a small curved knife. He uses a small spoon to clean the artichokes thoroughly, leaving a round white disc of the inner flesh, then lovingly rubs them with salt and lemon juice one by one, finally throwing them into a bucket full of water and lemon juice. These artichokes in the bucket—the fruits of Sadık's daily labour—are displayed to passers-by as Sadık continues to work. When asked whether they change their colour if not sold by the end of the day, he smiles and says, "That does not happen here...every single artichoke gets sold." His cart is always in the same spot, year after year. When the artichoke season is over, he switches to selling watermelons. He admits that artichokes demand far more hard work than watermelons but are considerably more profitable. At some point he proudly adds that there are many foreigners among his customers and explains the widespread belief that a steady diet of artichokes for 40 days is the best cure for various ailments of the liver.

Towards the end of the season, Sadık goes to Çanakkale (on the Gallipoli peninsula in northwestern Turkey) briefly, as a temporary worker for the Dardanel processed foods factory. He peels artichokes for canning and like tens of other temporary workers, is given a place to stay and a monthly salary. He says that he peels 1,200 to 1,300 artichokes a day. Sometimes they hold contests and Sadık swears that a friend of his is capable of peeling 2,500 artichokes a day. Picturing Sadık and his friends as 'human machines' in an assembly line, one can understand how much his own modest business with that small cart and bucket full of artichokes must mean to him.

Peeling the artichokes with affection, Istanbul

Clockwise from top left Artichoke field, Urla, Izmir; Freshly picked artichokes; Peeled artichokes in lemon water

Artichokes Cooked in Olive Oil *Zeytinyağlı Enginar*
(Serves 4)

Ingredients

Extra virgin olive oil	125 ml
Onion	1, peeled and sliced
Granulated sugar	1 Tbsp
Potato	1, peeled and cut into 1-cm cubes
Carrots	2, peeled and cut into 1-cm cubes
Tomatoes	2, peeled and chopped
Salt	to taste
Frozen peas	3 Tbsp
Globe artichokes	4, peeled and cleaned
Lemon juice	extracted from 1 lemon

Method

- Put two-thirds of the olive oil in a shallow pan and cook the onion with sugar. Add the potato and carrots and then tomatoes and salt. Cover and cook over low heat for about 10 minutes. Add the peas and cook altogether for another 10 minutes. Transfer this mixture to a plate.
- In the same pan, heat the remaining olive oil and place the artichokes in. Slightly cook both sides then drizzle lemon juice and sprinkle salt over. Spoon the vegetable mixture onto the centre of the artichokes. Cover and leave to cook 20 minutes, until the artichokes are tender.
- Transfer to a serving plate and serve warm or cold as an appetiser or as a digestive after a main course.

CUCUMBERS *Salatalık* or *Hıyar*

Most of the baby cucumbers that are sold in the streets of Istanbul are advertised as "Çengelköy cucumbers" referring to a small village on the Asian shores of the Bosphorus, which has historically been famous for its superior cucumbers. As small as fingers, they are so fresh and crisp that one cannot help eating a couple of them on the spot without bothering to peel or slice. Fresh from the vegetable gardens of the Marmara region, the Aegean and the Mediterranean, these baby cucumbers still carry the wilted flower on one end as a much appreciated sign of their freshness, to such an extent that in the Turkish language, the phrase *çiçeği burnunda* (literally "its flower on its nose") refers to anything that is young and fresh, from cucumbers and courgettes (zucchinis) to young girls.

Sold by the kilogram rather than individually, fresh cucumbers appear on every dinner table in late spring and summer, either on their own or mixed with yoghurt for the refreshing salad, *cacık* (recipe on page 60), or mixed with tomatoes, peppers and onions for the classic shepherd's salad (*çoban salata*, recipe on page 107). Eating cucumbers in the street as an instant snack is another unique flavour of urban life in Turkey. As baby cucumbers give way to larger cucumbers, street carts appear with loads of them ready for on-the-spot consumption. Once a customer picks the cucumber that he or she desires, the cucumber seller peels it carefully, removing the skin in long thin strips, then cuts the cucumber in half longitudinally

and sprinkles salt on both pieces before handling it to the eagerly waiting customer. While *"salatalık"* (literally "for the salad") is the more polite word for this popular produce, *"hıyar"* is also widely used, designating not just a cucumber but also (and no one knows why), referring to a rude and unpolished person in slang.

STRAWBERRIES *Çilek*

Strawberries *(çilek)* appear for only a couple of weeks in the spring, announcing their arrival with a strong, delicious fragrance. They are used extensively in desserts, jams, cakes and ice cream, yet there is no rival to the superb taste of these organically grown fresh strawberries eaten on their own, perhaps with a sprinkle of icing (confectioners') sugar. So far, Turkish streets seem to be blissfully uninterested in the large but bland tasting and artificially modified hothouse strawberries that one finds in the supermarkets of Europe and the United States. They would rather have the full satisfaction of eating real strawberries, albeit only for short few weeks. A smaller, pinkish variety known as the Ottoman strawberry *(Osmanlı çileği)* is sold only in straw baskets along the Bosphorus in Istanbul, displayed on the trucks that bring them from local gardens. Extremely delicate and difficult to handle without crushing, but unmatched in terms of its sweetness and superb fragrance, this variety is the top choice of those who wish to prepare strawberry jam.

From top Çengelköy cucumbers; Fresh strawberries in season, Istanbul

Cucumbers with Yoghurt *Cacık*
(Serves 4)

Ingredients

Cucumbers	4, small
Yoghurt	500 g
Garlic	4 cloves, peeled
Dill	1 bunch, chopped + 1 sprig for garnish
Salt	to taste
Ice cubes	

Method

• Wash the cucumbers and peel them if they are large with thick skin. (The very small, garden fresh cucumbers in Turkey do not need peeling.) Cut them into 0.5-cm cubes and place in a bowl. Add the yoghurt.

• Pass the garlic through a garlic press and add to the bowl. Add the dill and salt and mix well. You can add some water if you prefer a thinner *cacik*.

• Serve in individual bowls, garnished with dill sprigs and ice cubes.

Locally grown cucumbers, Çengelköy, Istanbul

Cucumber/Feta Cheese Spread
Salatalık ve Beyaz Peynir Ezmesi

(Makes 1 bowl)

Ingredients

Feta cheese	250 g
Extra virgin olive oil	3 Tbsp
Lemon juice	extracted from 1 lemon
Cucumbers	5, small, tips removed, coarsely chopped
Parsley (optional)	1 bunch, finely chopped
Paprika	a pinch

Method

- If the feta cheese is salty or too hard in texture, soak it in cold water for about 1 hour. Drain and place in a bowl, then add the olive oil and lemon juice and mash with the back of a spoon. Add the cucumbers and parsley if desired.
- Spread on toasted bread or on *simit* (a round sesame bagel) that can be bought in every street in Turkey. Sprinkle with paprika as a final accent.

MEATBALLS *Köfte*

Köfte is the generic Turkish word for various meatballs, patties or 'hamburgers' made primarily with finely ground meat. but mixed in some regional cuisines with lentils, bulgur and other grains. There are so many different *köfte* dishes in Turkish cuisine that an accurate count is unavailable. Ayşe Baysal gives the details and nutritious properties of 23 kinds and mentions that the city of Malatya in central Turkey by itself boasts some 64 different kinds.[1] The common grilled *köftes* are indispensable items in every picnic; *kadınbudu köfte* (meat and rice patties) are an all-time favourite of children and *izmir köfte* (served in tomato sauce) is standard fare of school cafeterias. There is even a spicy 'butcher's *köfte*' *(kasap köftesi)* that neighbourhood butchers prepare themselves and sell for immediate grilling or broiling. The skills that go into making and selling *köftes* must have made an impression in Turkish culture over time, as evidenced by the common expression, *köftehor*, in the Turkish language, used to refer (often with affection) to an able, manipulative or entrepreneurial person who manages to get his/her way in various situations.

Clockwise from top left A hungry customer waiting for his *köfte*; A smoky gathering—*köfte* carts in Eminönü, Istanbul; *Köftes* on skewers, Urfa

The largest concentration of Istanbul's *köfte* sellers is in Eminönü, a historical urban space surrounded by the Valide Sultan Mosque *(Yeni Cami)*, passenger ferry stops and the entrance to Istanbul's legendary Spice Bazaar. On a busy midday when all *köfte* stands are in full business, the scene resembles the aftermath of a great fire, with thick smoke rising in the air. The smell of grilled meat reaches potential customers from blocks away, and tourists of all nationalities, university students in groups and Istanbulites of all ages and classes patronise the *köfte* stands lined up along the square, giving this unique urban space its characteristic hustle and bustle.

Perhaps the most eccentric *köfte* seller in Istanbul is an elderly gentleman whose delicious *içli köftes* (recipe on page 67), a traditional food item in the regional cuisines of central and southern Turkey, are famous among the night crowds of Beyoğlu where cinemas, trendy cafes and jazz bars are located. Emerging in the late afternoon, he caters to the busy pedestrian traffic, offering a cheap, tasty and clean meal to Istanbulites on the go. Always dressed in his spotless and crisply ironed white shirt, and always serving his *içli köftes* from under a clean white cloth, he is known to his regular customers as 'doctor'. Without any of the noisy commotion with which street sellers typically sell their wares, he is quietly stationed in the same spot every evening, year after year, like a permanent fixture. One cannot help thinking that patronising his *içli köfte* stand is a privilege rather than an ordinary purchase.

Left *İçli köfte*, late night in Beyoğlu, Istanbul

Meat Loaf *Dalyan Köfte*
(Makes 1 loaf)

Ingredients

Ground (minced) beef	1.5 kg
Onion	1, medium, peeled and grated
Eggs	2
Breadcrumbs	90 g
Parsley	1 bunch
Salt and ground black pepper	to taste
Extra virgin olive oil	2 Tbsp
Ground cumin	1 tsp

Stuffing

Carrots	4, peeled and cut into 1-cm cubes
Potatoes	4–5, medium, peeled and cut into 1-cm cubes
Peas	250 g
Salt and ground black pepper	
Eggs	5, hardboiled and shelled
Extra virgin olive oil	4 Tbsp
Garlic	4 cloves, peeled and mashed
Tomato paste	2 Tbsp

Method

- Put all the ingredients except the stuffing into a deep bowl and mix well by hand. Transfer the mixture to an aluminium sheet about 30 x 40 cm and spread with a spatula or your hands, making a "slab" of meat. Cover and let it rest in the refrigerator.
- The size of the carrot and potato cubes should match the size of the peas. Steam the carrots until tender and deep-fry the potatoes. If using frozen peas, steam and combine with the carrots and potatoes. Season with salt and pepper.
- Take the meat spread out of the refrigerator. Spoon about half of the vegetable mixture onto the slab of meat, spreading it in the form of a strip closer to one side. Place the hardboiled eggs in the middle of this mixture, end to end. Carefully start rolling the meat slab with the help of the aluminium foil, to enclose the vegetable-egg mixture. Form a smooth log and remove the aluminium sheet.
- In another bowl, mix the olive oil, mashed garlic and tomato paste and spread on the meat log with a pastry brush. Cover with an aluminium sheet again and cook in a preheated oven at 175°C for 1 hour in a shallow roasting pan. In the last 5 minutes, spoon the rest of the vegetable mix into the side of the pan to warm.
- Remove the pan from the oven and let the meat loaf rest for 10 minutes before slicing, otherwise the slices may fall apart.
- Remove the aluminium sheet and spoon the extra vegetable mix to a bowl. Slice the log carefully and serve garnished with the additional vegetable mix.

Içli Köfte (Meat and Bulgur Patties)
(Makes approximately 20 pieces)

Ingredients

Fine bulgur	500 g
Ground (minced) lean beef	300 g
Salt and ground black pepper	
Water	500 ml
Plain (all-purpose) flour	1 Tbsp

Stuffing

Vegetable oil	1 Tbsp
Ground (minced) beef	300 g
Salt and ground black pepper	
Onion	1, peeled and cut into small cubes
Chilli flakes	1 tsp
Walnuts	100 g. chopped
Parsley	½ bunch, chopped

Method

- Prepare the stuffing. In a pan add the oil, ground beef, salt and pepper. Start cooking over medium heat. Add the onion and cook for 10 minutes until the meat is well done. Add the chilli flakes and the walnuts. Mix well. Remove from the heat and add chopped parsley. Set aside.

- If you have a mixer with a dough hook, you will save a lot of time and energy. Put the bulgur and the ground beef in a bowl. Add salt and pepper and start mixing by hand or with a mixer. Add water as you go. The only trick in this recipe is to knead the mixture for as long as possible, otherwise the meat patties will crumble when you start boiling them.

- Add the flour to help the dough to stick together. It should take about 20 minutes of kneading in a mixer and about 1 hour by hand. When ready, take enough mixture to fill your palm. Flatten it by hand and put about 1 Tbsp of the stuffing in the centre. Enclose and shape by hand into a ball. When they are ready, bring a pot of water to boil, add salt, and cook the meat patties for 20 minutes. Once the water comes back to the boil, leave to simmer and stir gently from time to time. Remove from the pot with a strainer and keep aside.

- Serve freshly boiled for a lighter, healthier dish. Alternatively, serve the traditional way by deep-frying until golden brown.

Kadınbudu Köfte (Meat and Rice Patties)
(Serves 4)

Ingredients

Ground (minced) beef	500 g
Cooked rice	250 g
Salt and ground black pepper	
Eggs	2
Onion	1, medium, peeled and grated
Parsley	1 bunch, chopped
Plain (all-purpose) flour	3 Tbsp
Breadcrumbs	
Cooking oil for frying	

Method

- Put the ground beef in a bowl with the rice, salt and pepper, 1 egg, grated onion and the chopped parsley. Mix well with your hands and shape into rounded or oval meat patties. Place on a plate.
- Spread the flour on a large plate and spread the breadcrumbs on another plate. Beat the remaining egg in a bowl. Dip the meat patties first into the flour, coat well and shake off excess flour. Then dip them into the egg and finally coat with the breadcrumbs.
- Heat the oil for frying and fry the meat patties for about 2 minutes on each side until golden brown. Drain on absorbent paper and serve.

Meatball Soup *Ekşili Köfte*
(Serves 4)

Ingredients

Ground (minced) lean beef	500 g
Rice	170 g
Water	125 ml
Parsley	$\frac{1}{2}$ bunch, chopped
Salt and ground black pepper	to taste
Onion	1, medium, peeled and grated
Plain (all-purpose) flour	3 Tbsp

Liaison

Egg yolks	2
Lemon juice	extracted from 1 lemon

Method

- Combine all the ingredients, except for the flour and liaison, in a bowl and mix well. Shape the mixture into small balls, slightly bigger than hazelnuts.
- Spread the flour onto a tray and transfer the meatballs to the tray, shaking and coating them thoroughly. Do not shake off the excess flour. Set the coated meatballs aside.
- In a deep pot, bring 1.5 litres of water to the boil and add salt according to taste. Lower in the meatballs. When the water comes back to the boil, reduce the heat and simmer the meatballs for 30–35 minutes until the rice is totally cooked. Stir occasionally with soft movements, do not break the meatballs.
- When the meatballs are ready, mix the egg yolks and lemon juice in a small bowl. Temper with the liquid of the soup, and then return the liaison to the pot. Cook for a further 3 minutes and remove from heat. Spoon into bowls and serve sprinkled with chilli flakes.

GRILLED LIVER KEBABS *Ciğer Kebap*

Although grilled or sautéed liver is a popular dish throughout many parts of Turkey, eating grilled liver kebabs *(ciğer kebap)* early in the morning is a regional eccentricity that one can see only in the streets of Urfa and Gaziantep in southeastern Turkey. Calf liver is the preferred ingredient for this *kebap* (generic word designating grilled items) but grilling spleen, heart and lungs is also quite common in the region. Typically, livers or lungs are diced and arranged on skewers, with alternating pieces of animal fat to make the *kebap* softer and juicier. *Ciğer kebap* sellers position themselves on busy streets for a daily ritual starting around 5 am and continuing until about 10 am.

For most people, the idea of breakfast would hardly ever include such an unlikely item as grilled liver, yet the regulars of these *kebap* stands insist that it is not at all as a heavy breakfast as one may think. And since it is believed to enhance red blood cells in the body, they consider it a particularly healthy start to the day. In most places, the skewers of liver are placed on rectangular coal grills lined up along the sidewalks. When they are thoroughly cooked, the grilled pieces are wrapped in thin bread with parsley, mint, chilli peppers and onions. In Adana, the liver is sprinkled with cumin before being wrapped.

Watching the *ciğer kebap* rituals of the Southeast is a curious and appetising experience. In Gaziantep, for example, one is attracted to the *ciğer kebap* stands in front of the stone walls of an old mansion by the sensory indicators that are hard to miss: intense smoke rising from the grills and the strong aromatic smell of sizzling animal fat. Around each grill, one finds a small crowd of people, the customers indistinguishable from the sellers because everyone is equally busy turning the skewers over the coal fire or preparing their wraps. Each stand has its local regulars who display the ease of people moving around in their own kitchens. With a quick glance at the prepared skewers, these regular customers select the ones they want and place them on the grill themselves. Surrounded by the intense smoke, they attend to their own skewers and carefully prepare their own wraps to suit their tastes. Grabbing a bottle of *ayran* from the cooler behind, they finally proceed to eat their wraps with a conspicuously big appetite whetted by the smell and the smoke.

With a historical predilection for meat dishes and a high consumption of lamb and beef in traditional Turkish cuisine, especially in central and eastern Anatolia, it is not surprising that almost no part of the animal gets discarded. Sautéed lamb kidneys *(böbrek sote)*, tripe soup *(işkembe çorbası)*, 'brain salad' in lemon juice and olive oil *(beyin salatası)*, stew of lambs' feet *(paça)* and even grilled lamb's head (*kelle*, see page 152) are popular dishes in many restaurants. Of these, an indispensable accompaniment to *rakı* drinking is the so-called 'Albanian liver' (still bearing the legacy of a vast multi-cultural empire), one of the tastiest traditional Turkish mezes *(arnavut ciğer)*. For those unconcerned about cholesterol levels, the recipe follows on page 72.

Itinerant liver seller, early 20th century (Istanbul Metropolitan Municipality, Atatürk Library)

From top 6 am, breakfast time in Gaziantep; Grilled liver kebabs, Gaziantep

Albanian Liver *Arnavut Ciğeri*

(Serves 4)

Ingredients

Lamb's liver	500 g, washed
Plain (all-purpose) flour	5 Tbsp
Salt	to taste
Vegetable oil for frying	
Paprika	1 tsp
Chilli flakes	1 tsp
Dried mint	1 tsp

Method

- Peel and remove the outer membrane of the liver with the help of a sharp knife. Dice the liver into 2-cm pieces.
- Put the flour in a plastic bag or spread on a plate. Add the salt and mix well. Coat the liver pieces with flour by shaking in the bag or rolling on the plate.
- Heat the oil in a frying pan (skillet). Shake off the excess flour and fry the liver pieces until golden brown. The liver pieces should be well cooked but the centre should still be juicy.
- To serve, sprinkle with paprika, chilli flakes and mint. It is also customary to serve this dish accompanied with chopped red onions mixed with ground *sumac* (sumak, a slightly sour tasting red spice), cubed tomatoes, chopped parsley and chillies.

Chickpea wrap, midday at a market in Gaziantep

Milk pudding and *aşure*, Adana

CHICKPEA WRAP *Nohut Dürüm*

The wholesale fresh produce market of Gaziantep (a major city in southeastern Turkey) is in Samanpazarı (literally "Haymarket"), adjacent to a flea market and occupying the grounds of an old cemetery. The fruit and vegetable dealers of the market proudly announce that they are members of the World Fresh Produce Markets Association.

The chickpea wrap *(nohut dürüm)* seller is a familiar figure in the market, conducting his business from the same spot in the same way for many years. His customers come to the market from many different parts of the city. He explains how he soaks the chickpeas overnight and cooks them until soft and mushy. In the past, when butchers were more generous donating bones to him, he used to cook his chickpeas in bone stock for better flavour. Now, he has to purchase the bones, he laments bitterly. Before wrapping the chickpeas in thin bread, he adds parsley, onions and chilli, then he serves the wrap with *ayran*. He says that he sells a huge pot of chickpeas in a few hours; without doubt, the wraps make a very economical and nutritious meal.

MILK PUDDING *Muhallebi*

In one of the side streets of Adana, visitors to the city come across a clean and shiny cart selling the popular milk pudding of Turkey called *muhallebi*. The owner, Doğan Ocak, explains that he is new in this business. After losing his former job in Turkey's recent economic crisis, he decided to turn his wife's culinary skills into profit, especially her delicious *muhallebi* and *aşure*. He sells about 20–30 puddings a day which his wife prepares at home. It is evident that Mr Ocak is not a seasoned street seller. Without the shrill screams of other sellers announcing their wares, he stands quietly in one corner, looking less like the seller of the puddings than a potential customer.

The puddings are another story: they are absolutely delicious and unmistakably homemade! Best of all, he serves them not in disposable plastic containers, but in glass bowls, better fit for a restaurant than a street stand. As one retreats to a shady corner to eat a bowl of this delicious *muhallebi*, one cannot help recalling the famous verses of Orhan Veli, a prominent modern Turkish poet. In *Promise (Söz)*, he invites a young and attractive woman for an intimate rendezvous at the *muhallebi* shop *(muhallebici)* during the busiest time of the day. This is only one poetic reminder of the prominence of milk pudding shops in the urban culture and collective consciousness of modern Turkey.

Savouring a milk pudding in the heat of Adana

Assorted milk puddings, Adana

AŞURE

Aşure is a traditional rich pudding made from a base of wheat and sugar, to which many ingredients are added such as beans, nuts and dried fruit. In popular culture, it is believed that the origin of *aşure* is somewhat 'biblical', traced to the Great Flood and the story of Noah's Ark. Having almost run out of food, the inhabitants of the ark decide to create a dish by mixing whatever was left at the bottom of sacks and barrels thereby producing the first *aşure*! It is, however, under the Islamic faith—especially by the Shiites and the mystic orders of Sufism—that *aşure* has acquired its traditional symbolism and ritualistic significance.

In the Islamic tradition, *aşure* is prepared two times in a year. The first is during the month of Muharram to commemorate the 7th century massacre of Imam Hüseyin in Karbala (today's Iraq), a historic event of great significance and sanctity for the Shiites. The second is called *Sefer aşuresi* (*sefer* meaning military campaign) to celebrate Imam Zeynelabidin's escape from the Karbala massacre to continue the dynasty of the Prophet. The former symbolises mourning and pain while the latter represents a festive and happy occasion.[2] During the Ottoman period, in Istanbul's 900 lodges of religious orders, both Muharram and *Sefer aşure* were prepared and distributed according to established rituals. Today, *Sefer aşuresi* has largely been forgotten, while cooking the Muharrem *aşuresi* is a popular tradition, not just among the Shiite and Alevi communities, but also among the predominantly Sunni Muslims of Turkey.

In Sufi rituals (mystic orders of Anatolia), the preparation and consumption of *aşure* is a form of prayer in itself with deep symbolic meanings. Every ingredient going into the *aşure* cauldron should be added raw, slowly "boiled", "matured" and "calmed down" in the process, analogous to life itself. *Aşure* should be prepared on a Saturday, cooked on a Sunday and ritualistically eaten on a Tuesday. Historical records tell us that all the expenses and ingredients of *aşure* preparation in the religious lodges *(tekkeler)* were provided by the Ottoman State via the pious endowments *(vakıflar)*.[3] Believed to be a holy and therapeutic dessert, it was distributed to the rest of the community. In many places, the custom continues even today.

Aşure (Serves 8)

Ingredients

Chickpeas	50 g
Dry white beans	60 g
Whole wheat	100 g
Salt	½ tsp
Granulated sugar	350 g
Chestnuts	500 g
Rice	55 g
Lemon or orange zest	from 1 lemon or orange
Pear	1, small, peeled and sliced
Apple	1, peeled and sliced
Dried sour cherries	20 g
Dried apricots and dried figs	50 g each, cut in quarters
Red currants and sultanas	a handful each
Pine nuts	a handful

Topping

Pomegranate seeds
Ground cinnamon
Shredded coconut
Ground pistachios

Method

- Soak the chickpeas and white beans in cold water overnight. The next day, place 2 litres water in a large pot and start cooking the soaked chickpeas and white beans, along with the whole wheat, salt and sugar. Cook for about 2 hours until tender.

- As the above ingredients simmer on low heat, slit the chestnuts and boil them in another pot for a short time, then rinse and peel them. Be careful not to overcook the chestnuts: you want them in whole pieces.

- Add the rice, zest and all the other ingredients, except the topping, one by one into the simmering pot of chickpeas and white beans. Adjust the sugar according to taste and cook for a further 15 minutes. It is important to stir occasionally, to prevent the ingredients from sticking to the bottom of the pot.

- Aşure will get thicker as it cools so the amount of water can also be adjusted according to taste. Once it cools a little, portion it to dessert plates and top with pomegranate seeds, ground cinnamon, shredded coconut and ground pistachios.

Baked Rice Pudding *Fırın Sütlaç*
(Serves 4)

Ingredients

Milk	1 litre
Vanilla bean	1
Rice	170 g
Salt	½ tsp
Granulated sugar	200 g

Method

- Place the milk in a saucepan. Cut the vanilla bean into half and scrape the seeds. Bring the milk to the boil then remove from the heat. Put the vanilla pod and seeds in and let it infuse for 10 minutes. Remove the pod.
- Place the rice into a pot with water just enough to cover it. Add the salt and bring to the boil. Simmer until the water is absorbed. Add the milk and the sugar and bring to the boil again. Let it simmer, with the lid closed until the rice is totally cooked and mushy. This will take about 45 minutes. Pour into individual serving cups.
- Heat the oven to 150°C and brown the tops of the puddings for about 5 minutes. As it cools, the pudding will get thicker so do not be alarmed if it is runny at this stage.

TAŞ KADAYIF ('Pancake' Dessert)

Kadayıf is the generic word for dough-based desserts soaked in sweet syrup. These popular and traditional desserts of Turkish cuisine come in different shapes and are named accordingly. The flat *kadayıf (yassi kadayıf)* is a kind of round crumpet about 10 cm in diameter, deep-fried and then soaked in syrup. The shredded wheat or literally wire *kadayıf (tel kadayıf)* is produced by a more elaborate traditional process that is delightful to watch, especially in the old market of Antakya, the ancient Antioch close to the Syrian border, where shredded wheat desserts like *künefe* are famous local specialties. Making the shredded wheat is an art that requires special equipment and talent. By turning on a small tap attached to a large metal bucket containing liquid dough, the dough is drizzled onto a large and slowly rotating hot griddle surface. Cooking almost instantly into crisp, continuous 'wires', the dough shreds are gathered into bundles as the liquid dough continues to flow for a new round.

Taş kadayıf is a special, local variety of flat *kadayıf* that one can find in Antakya. To make the *taş kadayıf*, liquid dough is slowly poured onto the hot griddle to make small, round pancakes of about 5–6 cm diameter. When these 'pancakes' rise and turn golden brown, they are removed from the griddle and a filling of ground walnuts and sugar is sandwiched between every two pancakes. These layered pancakes are fried first and then soaked in sweet syrup. Traditionally, warm *taş kadayıfs* were served with a drizzle of molasses *(pekmez)* diluted with water. Nowadays, a thick syrup of sugar and water has replaced the molasses.

KÜNEFE (Shredded Wheat Dessert)

After watching the making of *tel kadayıf*, it is time for the most famous specialty of the Antakya region, the *künefe* dessert. In the old market, the *künefe* master demonstrates this local 'art' with swift and skillful movements. He heaps the shredded wheat onto a large round copper tray, breaking and mixing the shreds for a long time. This is probably the most elaborate and skill-demanding step of the whole procedure, akin to fluffing and airing heaps of wool to give them a light, airy texture before filling a mattress or a pillow. When the *künefe* is finally done, the master pours melted butter over it and places the tray on the stove, continuing to break the shreds until they are ready for shaping. At that point, setting aside half of the heap, he spreads and flattens the other half into a large round disc. He does this with remarkable skill and speed, using his knife as a spreader as he keeps rotating the tray continuously over the heat. Next, he spreads a layer of fresh cheese made from cow's milk over the flattened disc of shredded wheat while he explains that the *künefe* in Istanbul can never match the superior taste of Antakya *künefes* because this particular cheese is not always available there. As the last step, he spreads the remaining half of the shredded wheat over the cheese and flattens it, sandwiching the cheese between the two layers. When the bottom layer has turned golden brown, he uses an identical tray to turn the entire disc upside down and completes the cooking process. After this, the dessert is sweetened by a generous amount of syrup made of sugar and water. The syrup is prepared in advance and cooled to room temperature. Rather than pouring the syrup over the entire tray at once, he pours it incrementally over each portion of the dessert as customers arrive. This way he prevents the *künefe* from getting soggy. As he serves his customers from the warm tray, he is already working on a new tray for the next batch.

From top *Taş kadayıf*, Adana; *Künefe*, Antakya

A field of red poppies

BICI BICI (Starch-based Dessert)

This very simple and unusual dessert (with an unusual name) is an extremely popular and widely consumed item in the region of Adana in southern Turkey. Although each seller may adopt small variations in the presentation and serving of *bici bici*, the basic idea is the same everywhere: a kind of stiff jelly, about 2-cm thick, made of water and corn flour (cornstarch). As a customer approaches, the *bici bici* seller removes a piece of this white jelly from the tray, cuts it into small cubes and arranges them on a serving plate. He sprinkles them with icing (confectioners') sugar, a handful of ice shavings (by picking up a piece of ice and grating it directly onto the plate) and adds more icing sugar. He then drizzles a few drops of rose water over and as a final touch, pours a generous amount of sweet red syrup (a mixture of sugar, water and food colouring) on top. A mouth-watering treat!

After each serving, the ice container is carefully covered. The source of the ice, the crucial ingredient of *bici bici*, has changed over time. Long ago, the ice was brought from the peaks of the Taurus Mountains along Turkey's southern coast. The snow from the lower areas was shovelled into trucks and transported to the city. This procedure has now been replaced with commercially produced ice blocks purchased from ice manufacturers. Another story about *bici bici* is that the red syrup that completes the dessert, originally received its fascinating colour from the petals of red poppies. Although plausible (endless fields of red poppies abound in the region), none of Adana's *bici bici* sellers use poppies or remember anyone using them.

A cooling plate of *bici bici*, Adana

'Machine aesthetic': *Atom gazoz* fountain, Gaziantep

SODA FOUNTAIN *Atom Gazoz*

The soda fountains *(atom gazoz)* in the streets of Gaziantep and Adana work on similar principles. They are actually small scale, mobile soda factories. The primitive 'industrial aesthetic' of the shiny metal water tank and the pipes, the luxury of finding delicious, cold soda within easy reach as one crosses the street on a hot day and above all, the special taste and the unbelievably cheap price of the soda, take one through a journey in time. While most of Turkey's 'street foods' are items grown or prepared elsewhere, *atom gazoz* is a unique example of on-site production, not to mention the fact that it is a kind of technological production, albeit a primitive and outdated one!

In Adana, Mehmet Bey has been making and selling *atom gazoz* for 40 years. His metal fountain has two heads: one for cherry-flavoured concentrate and the other for cola flavoured concentrate. When a customer approaches, he picks up a glass, rinses it with water from the water tank, fills it halfway with flavoured concentrate according to the customer's choice and finally tops it with bubbly carbonated water from the other tank. Ready to go! The price of a glass of flavoured soda is about one-fifth of branded and commercially packaged sodas of similar taste. This is certainly one of the factors that make street sodas so attractive. Yet, it is certainly not the only reason for the

popularity of *atom gazoz* as addicts to its taste would testify. As Mehmet Bey pushes his cart into his usual street corner on a spring afternoon, a regular customer, Ferit Bey, appears as he has done every afternoon for many years. He is over 70 years old. He says he has been drinking the same soda since his childhood and is incurably addicted to the taste. To tease the seller-turned-friend, he adds that as Mehmet Bey gets older and his shaky hands lose their accuracy in preparing the mix, the sodas seem to taste sweeter and better. Mehmet Bey announces, without regrets, that none of his children will continue the traditional business; he wants them to go to university. It is not hard to see that this is probably the last generation for street sodas.

As one observes the customers drinking their sodas and chatting with the soda sellers of Adana, one cannot help wondering why a generic beverage (flavoured soda) consumed everywhere in the world is produced and sold in this particular way only in this region. The heat may be one plausible explanation, but many parts of Turkey are similarly hot without a single *atom gazoz* seller in sight! One can speculate that perhaps they existed in other parts of the country in the past, but gradually lost out to commercially packaged sodas.

Atom gazoz seller in his usual corner, Adana

SHERBETS (FRUIT COOLERS)
Şerbet

Different kinds of fruit sherbets constitute a widely consumed and thirst quenching traditional Turkish beverage. Once upon a time, sherbets were also prepared in homes, in addition to being sold in candy shops or at street stands during the summer months. The wandering sherbet sellers, with glasses tucked into their specially designed belts, used to announce their arrival with loud cries, *"Buz gibi şerbet var—otuziki dişe keman çaldırıyor!"* ("Ice cold sherbet—will cause your thirty-two teeth to chatter with cold!") Others prefer to make a kind of clinking "music" with their glasses. Although increasingly less common in other parts of the country, the sherbet tradition is still alive and well in the densely populated cities of southeastern Turkey.

A wide range of sherbets is mentioned in Abdi Musa's treatise (1429–1430) on the food culture and eating and drinking habits of the time. Some of these exotic varieties include sherbets of fresh sour cherries, plums of different kinds, fresh and dried pears and sweet grapes.[4] Fruit coolers also appear in the memoirs of Hagop Mintzuri, who narrates his childhood memories of the sherbet shop in Beşiktaş, Istanbul in the early 20th century.[5] In these memoirs stretching back to the years before the commercial availability of ice, it is narrated that two Albanian sherbet sellers/makers, Eşref and Zeynel, stocked heaps of winter snow in their basement, covered with hay and wood chips to prevent melting. They made sherbets of strawberry, sour cherry, lemon and grape, poured them into shiny brass pitchers and carried these pitchers to the market on their backs to sell by the glass. In winter months, they switched to making/selling *boza* and *sahlep*.

A rarer and more special kind of sherbet called *demirhindi şerbeti*, made from tamarind *(hint hurması)* is an all-time favourite among sherbet drinkers. The famous *demirhindi serbeti* of Hacı Bekir, famous Istanbul confectioners since the 18th century, can still be purchased today. Ahmet Haşim, prominent Turkish author and poet of the early 20th century, talks about the *demirhindi şerbeti* as "one of the special tastes and smells, one of the unrivalled small pleasures, small details, small joys that make a country a homeland".[6]

Refreshing orange sherbet, Adana

Lohusa **Sherbet** *Lohusa Şerbeti*

A special kind of sherbet served cold or hot is the *lohusa şerbeti*. It is traditionally prepared after childbirth to symbolise fertility, to endow the mother with ample breast milk and to wish the newborn a healthy and happy life. Although it is a gradually disappearing tradition, in many Turkish households, *lohusa şerbeti* is still offered to guests on their first visit to a new mother after childbirth. The idea is to celebrate the start of a new life with a sweet taste. The sherbet is made by boiling *nöbet şekeri*, a red-coloured candy, with cinnamon, cloves and sweet-smelling herbs. Although a simple beverage, *lohusa şerbeti* attracts one with its pretty red colour, its pleasant smell and above all, its association with a happy occasion. For most Turks, it is a beverage that immediately brings to mind the joyful guest traffic in a house after childbirth and the warm atmosphere filled with happy conversations, especially among women.

Lohusa sherbet

SUMMER

Pomegranates, cherries, apricots, mulberries, peaches and grapes come out in that order from June well into October, making summer a heavenly season for delicious fresh fruits.

Long days and warm evenings coupled with school vacations make street life especially colourful during the summer. Ice cream sellers appear in the streets tempting children and adults alike. Pomegranates *(nar)*, cherries *(kiraz)*, apricots *(kayısı)*, mulberries *(dut)*, peaches *(seftali)* and grapes *(üzüm)* come out in that order from June well into October, making summer a heavenly season for delicious fresh fruits. Sour cherries *(visne)*, which are widely consumed in Turkey for everything from desserts and compotes to sherbets and ice cream, also come out in July. Watermelons arrive in trucks and carts everywhere. Vegetables compete with fruits on street stands; tomatoes, green peppers and aubergines (eggplants) are sold in huge quantities since most summer dishes and salads use some, if not all of these three basic ingredients. Spraying fruits and vegetables with pesticides or 'genetically engineering' them is still not very widespread in Turkey; nor is early picking for better transportation a common practice. As a result, fruits and vegetables are mostly organic, ripe and absolutely delicious.

Life slows down a little bit in the summer as a result of the heat, but as soon as the sun loses its intensity, entire urban populations pour out into the street and stay outside well into the night. The so-called 'tea gardens' *(çay bahçesi)* where tea, Turkish coffee, cold beverages, *ayran* and ice cream are served, are often packed full. Restaurants make good business in the summer and alcohol consumption becomes conspicuous. Crowds of people take late afternoon or evening walks, often nibbling on sunflower seeds or licking ice cream cones. The primary purpose of such purposeless promenading is to see and be seen. Others prefer to sit on their front steps for the same purpose. In the majority of urban households, dinner is eaten out on the balcony and since densely packed apartment buildings constitute the major residential pattern in Turkish cities, dining table conversations, music or TV in the background and the sounds of eating and drinking mix into each other, filling the evening air with a continuous urban chatter. The smells are equally significant in setting the mood of summer evenings: the appetising smell of fried aubergines and peppers with garlic yoghurt, the distinct anise smell of the *rakı* tables often accompanied by fragrant melons, and the pervasive smoky smell of the kebabs are the most characteristic of these summer sensations.

Opposite, clockwise from top left Cucumbers and mulberries, Çengelköy, Istanbul; 'Seeds' of the exotic pomegranate; Pomegranates for sale, Adana; Glass of pomegranate juice; Garden fresh tomatoes, Levent, Istanbul

Ice cream seller on Adana-Mersin highway

ICE CREAM *Dondurma*

The idea of eating ice cream as a dessert and throughout the whole year is a very recent phenomenon in Turkey. It is largely a result of the influx of attractively packaged imported ice creams and their domestic counterparts that occupy entire aisles in large supermarkets. Some 20 years ago, an Istanbulite who desired to have ice cream during the winter had no choice but to travel all the way to Moda on the Asian side of Istanbul where the only year-round ice cream store was located. In those years, Turkish ice cream was rather primitive and unrefined. It came in a number of different colours (white for vanilla, brown for chocolate and pink for strawberry) but all three tasted more or less the same. In the last decade or so, triggered by competition from foreign brands, the quality of Turkish ice cream improved dramatically. Chain stores like Mado (short for Maraş Dondurması or Maraş Ice Cream, designating the origins of the enterprise in Maraş, southeastern Turkey) opened in major cities and regional flavours entered the mass-market, such as the exquisite pistachio ice cream of Mado. Nevertheless, for many Turks, the memories and tastes of the old time ice creams sold in street carts are still fresh: for example, the famous sour cherry ice cream sold in front of the Grand Club in Büyükada, the largest of the Prince Islands off the Marmara shores of Istanbul or the homemade *sahlep* ice creams of our grandmothers' time that have now disappeared. Still, when summer comes, it is not uncommon to spot an occasional ice cream cart, its wafer cones stacked high, passing by residential streets.

Helva Ice Cream *Helvalı Dondurma*
(Makes approximately 700 ml)

Ingredients

Milk	500 ml
Vanilla essence (extract)	
Egg yolks	4
Granulated sugar	100 g (optional)
Helva (tahini* bars, plain or with pistachio)	250 g, grated

Method

• Put the milk in a pan, stir in the vanilla essence and place it over heat. Bring it just before the boiling point and set aside.

• In a bowl, beat the egg yolks until creamy and pale. Add a few tablespoons of the vanilla milk and mix well. Transfer the tempered mixture to the pan of milk and mix well to avoid any lumps. Add sugar if desired and let it dissolve. (As the sweetness of this ice cream comes from the *helva*, you can adjust the amount of granulated sugar according to taste.)

• Bring a pot of water to simmer and place the pan over the water without letting the bottom touch the water. Mix continuously with a wooden spoon until it coats the back of the spoon. Do not bring the water to the boil or it will curdle.

• When ready, remove from the heat and mix the grated *helva* into the ice cream mixture. Stir until smooth, then cool in the refrigerator and transfer into an ice cream machine and churn according to the manufacturer's instructions. When the ice cream is ready, serve it with your choice of topping. Here, it is pictured topped with molasses.

* Tahini bars are made of toasted and ground sesame seeds. Combined with molasses *(pekmez)*, it makes an appetising and nutritious food for many Turks.

Sour Cherry Sorbet *Vişne Sorbe*
(Makes approximately 1 litre)

Ingredients

Sour cherries	1 kg, pitted
Granulated sugar	300 g
Lemon	1, juice extracted and zest grated
Egg whites	2, lightly beaten

Method

- Place the cherries in a pot and add the sugar, lemon juice and zest. Slowly bring to the boil and simmer for 5 minutes.
- When the mixture cools a little, pour the contents of the pot into a blender and blend thoroughly. After blending, it should measure about 1 litre. Transfer to a shallow pan and let it cool completely.
- Beat the egg whites into the cooled blended mixture and transfer to an ice cream machine. Churn according to the manufacturer's instructions.
- When the ice cream is ready, serve with a topping of sour cherry sauce.*

*Sour Cherry Sauce *Vişne Sosu*

Ingredients

Sour cherries	300 g, pitted
Campari	100 ml
Granulated sugar	3 Tbsp
Allspice	1 Tbsp

Method

- Put all the ingredients into a pot and bring to the boil. Simmer until it thickens and covers the back of a spoon as you lift it. When cooled, remove the allspice. The sauce can be stored refrigerated for 2 days, but if it is to be prepared in advance, note that it thickens further in the refrigerator.

Melon carts often display a single produce

SUMMER FRUITS

As summer arrives, the rich variety of fresh fruits turn the street stands into colourful displays that are as delightful to the eye as they are to the taste buds. Following the strawberries, mulberries, apricots, persimmons *(hurma)* and plum *(erik)* varieties are the most common fruits of the early summer, and they are also used extensively for jams, marmalades and compotes.

Mulberries of both white and purple varieties abound in Central Anatolia, the Marmara region and especially around Bursa, the traditional centre of the silk industry. In earlier times when large extended families lived in houses with gardens, harvesting mulberries was a joyous ritual: a large sheet was held from all corners by four people under the mulberry tree while a fifth person climbed the tree to shake it, making the ripe mulberries 'rain' onto the sheet. Apricots, grown extensively around Malatya in Central Anatolia, are everyone's favourite. Small in size but very sweet, they are the pride of Malatya where a whole apricot industry has developed, filling specialty shops with dried apricots, apricot pastes and jams, and even elegant bottles of apricot fragrances.

The best kind of peaches, the *yarma şeftali,* takes slightly longer to ripen, and they appear on street carts only a few weeks into the summer, as with the grapes. Conspicuously superior to other kinds of peaches, the thin skin of the *yarma şeftali* peels very easily, its flesh separates readily from the seed and its juiciness is without comparison. The progressive disappearance of the historical *yarma şeftali* orchards around Bursa (now a major centre for the automotive industry) is a sad episode illustrating the price of industry and progress in Turkey. A rich variety of grapes can be purchased on the streets, from the green, yellow and black seeded grapes from the vineyards of Aegean and western Anatolia to the very sweet and seedless Smyrna grapes (Izmir *üzümü*) from which the best golden raisins are produced.

Seedless Smyrna grapes, Aegean Coast

A persimmon stall in the streets of Adana

Although carts featuring a single produce are not uncommon, such as the melon carts, stacked with melons and watermelons *(kavun-karpuz)*, street sellers often display a colourful mix of summer fruits. A most eccentric seller, Ismet Bey, originally from Adıyaman in central Anatolia, is now selling fruits in one of the busiest intersections of metropolitan Adana, from 9 am to 10 pm every day. He admits to being some sort of an 'order freak', arranging his apricots and strawberries one by one into astonishingly neat rows. He believes that presentation is extremely important in attracting customers. Indeed, when he lights his gas lamp after sunset, the light falling on his neat rows of strawberries and apricots make an exquisite sight. When the summer is over, he switches to selling pistachios and chestnuts—the latter again arranged into perfectly neat rows. Naturally!

A young mulberry seller in the shade of a truck, Diyarbakır

Ismet Bey lighting his gas lamp, Adana

Raisin and Apricot Cookies *Kuru Üzüm ve Kayısılı Kurabiye*
(Makes 30–35 cookies)

Ingredients

Butter or margarine	200 g, softened at room temperature
Brown sugar	250 g
Egg	1
Dried apricots	75 g, chopped
Raisins	75 g
Grated orange zest	1 tsp
Plain (all-purpose) flour	300 g
Ground cinnamon	1 tsp
Baking powder	1 tsp

Method

- Mix the butter or margarine and the brown sugar using an electric mixer until well incorporated. Add the egg, dried apricots, raisins and orange zest. Add the flour, ground cinnamon and baking powder and mix them all well into a soft dough using your hands.
- Pick pieces of the dough and shape by hand into round cookies. Arrange them on a non-stick baking sheet. Bake in a preheated oven at 150°C, for 15–20 minutes until lightly browned.

Apricot Jam *Kayısı Reçeli*

Ingredients

Fresh apricots	1 kg, pitted, pits reserved
Granulated sugar	1 kg
Lemon juice	extracted from 1 lemon

Method

- Place the apricots in a pot. Cover with the sugar and let it rest at room temperature for 5–6 hours or overnight in the refrigerator.
- Place the pot over heat and let the sugar melt. Bring to the boil and reduce the heat. After 10–15 minutes, remove the apricots with a slotted spoon and let the liquid continue boiling until it thickens to a syrupy consistency.
- Meanwhile, crack the shells of the apricot pits and collect the seeds. Return the apricots to the pot together with the seeds for another 5 minutes. Add the juice of the lemon and remove from the heat. Transfer to a jar. Keeping the jar exposed to sunlight for a day or two will make the jam thicker.

Old woman selling tomatoes, Izmir

TOMATOES *Domates*

It is perhaps the dream of almost every retiree in Turkey to have a small garden patch to grow his or her own tomatoes. Although very few Turks can realise this dream, almost everyone knows and cherishes the incomparably superior taste of a garden fresh, ripe tomato, especially in recent years when 'engineered' hothouse tomatoes have invaded the market. The differences between the two are always astonishing. The 'real' tomatoes are red and juicy with very thin skins that peel off easily and are absolutely delicious. The others are photogenic but disappointing: mostly spongy, thick-skinned and still green inside (as a result of early picking to transport well). Fortunately for the Turks, the heaps of tomatoes that can be purchased from street sellers or in weekly neighbourhood markets are mostly real, ripe, large tomatoes brought in from local gardens when in season. Other kinds like plum or cherry tomatoes are rare in Turkey, but are becoming increasingly more available in gourmet grocery stores and supermarkets.

The tomato ranks as the highest consumed vegetable in Turkey. A rich source of vitamin C, it is the symbol of a healthy Mediterranean diet as also reflected in the language: a person with healthy pink cheeks is referred to as "tomato-cheeked". A summer salad is unthinkable without tomatoes. Typically, ripe tomatoes are peeled and diced to make shepherd's salad (*çoban salatası*, recipe on page 107) together with other ingredients like onions, peppers, mint and oregano. However, the best of the tomatoes are eaten alone or *söğüş* as it is called. Peeled, sliced and arranged on a plate, perhaps with a drizzle of olive oil. Being the basic and indispensable ingredient of so many dishes, soups and sauces, the tomato is always present in Turkish cuisine in some shape or form. When good fresh tomatoes are at their cheapest in mid summer, more traditional households take the time to preserve them for other seasons. The most common methods of preservation are sun-drying halved or quartered tomatoes and making tomato paste by squeezing fresh tomatoes through a fine mesh and leaving in the sun. Today, in most cities, such procedures have become distant memories, replaced by the commercial availability of a wide range of tomato products on supermarket shelves.

Fresh local tomatoes in a grocery store, Izmir

A cart full of fresh green peppers, Gaziantep

GREEN PEPPERS *Yeşil Biber*

Whether displayed with other vegetables or alone, heaps of fresh green peppers on stationary stands or mobile carts are familiar scenes of urban life in the summer. Long, thin and crisp green peppers *(sivri biber)* are as nutritious as they are delicious when eaten raw with some salt. While most customers try to single out the sweet ones from the heap, others like to add a few hot peppers to their summer salad to make it more appetising. Green bell peppers *(dolma biber)* that one finds abundantly in Turkey are smaller, thinner skinned and significantly more delicious compared to the ones found in most European and American supermarkets. They are typically used to prepare a stuffed pepper *(biber dolması)* dish, one of the most characteristic traditional dishes of Turkish cuisine, hence the name *dolma biber*. A third kind, thicker than *sivri biber* but thinner than *dolma biber* is a sweet variety known as *çarliston biber*. They are ideal for grilling and frying; their outer skins peel off very easily and the remaining flesh makes a delicious appetiser when mixed with garlic and yoghurt.

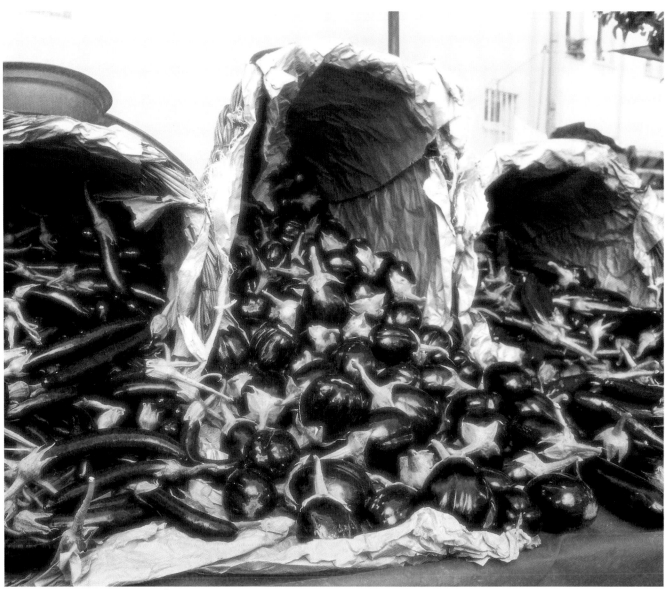

Varieties of aubergines in the street market, Ödemiş, Izmir

AUBERGINES (EGGPLANTS) *Patlıcan*

Aubergines are the centrepiece of traditional Turkish cuisine. Visitors to the country are often awed by the vast fields of aubergines, and the Turkish language contains numerous references to this pervasive vegetable in the form of riddles and idioms. Traced to prehistoric times in India, the aubergine is believed to have been transplanted to the Mediterranean basin around the 16th century. Its extensive use in Gaziantep cuisine in southeastern Turkey is legendary. Reluctant to go through a season without the aubergine, the people of Gaziantep dry the aubergine in large quantities for use in the winter.[1] Known for its appetite-inducing and artery-cleansing properties, and believed to be an effective remedy for indigestion, aubergine is used in over 200 Turkish dishes and delicacies, ranging from aubergine pickles to a most unlikely product—aubergine jam. Perhaps the most famous and traditional aubergine dish in Turkish cuisine is the *hünkar beğendi*, literally "The Sultan loved it!" Historical records trace the name of this dish to the reign of Sultan Abdülaziz (1861–1876), an Ottoman ruler with an especially large appetite who expected his Arab concubines to prepare and serve him special dishes. Ali Rıza Bey writes that one of these women, distinguished for her talent in preparing varieties of stuffed *(dolma)* vegetables, came up with this dish that earned great praise from the Sultan and hence its name![2]

Menemen (Eggs with Tomatoes and Peppers)
(Serves 4)

Ingredients

Butter	1 Tbsp
Onion	1, small, peeled, halved and thinly sliced
Green peppers	4, cored and sliced evenly
Yellow bell pepper	1, cored and sliced evenly
Red bell pepper	1, cored and sliced evenly
Tomatoes	3, peeled and cut into cubes
Salt and ground white pepper	
Parsley	1 bunch, chopped
Eggs	4

Method

- Melt the butter in a pan and add the onion. Cook over medium heat until the onion is tender. Add the peppers and cook together for a couple of minutes.
- Add the tomatoes and season with salt and pepper. Cook for another 5 minutes until the peppers and tomatoes are tender. Add the parsley and mix well. Break the eggs into the pan and cook until the egg whites are set but the yolks are still runny.

Shepherd's Salad *Çoban Salata*
(Serves 4)

Ingredients

Onion	1, medium, peeled and thinly sliced
Salt	
Tomatoes	3, medium
Cucumbers	4, tips cut and discarded
Parsley	¹/₂ bunch, coarsely chopped
Mint	¹/₂ bunch, coarsely chopped

Dressing

Lemon	¹/₂, juice extracted
Extra virgin olive oil	1 Tbsp
Pomegranate vinegar	1 Tbsp

Topping

Feta cheese	100 g, cut into cubes
Black olives	

Method

- Rub the onion well with salt, rinse and transfer to the salad bowl.
- Peel the tomatoes, then halve and cube them. Depending on the type of tomatoes, you may want to deseed them. Organically grown, local tomatoes in Turkey are usually very small and tasty so, it is very uncommon to remove the seeds.
- Cube the cucumbers to match the tomatoes. Again, depending on the type of cucumbers, peel as necessary. Turkish cucumbers are very fresh and small, so they are typically not peeled.
- Toss all the ingredients together and dress with the lemon juice, extra virgin olive oil, pomegranate juice and some salt. Top with cheese cubes and black olives before serving.

Dried aubergines for winter consumption. Gaziantep

Fried Aubergines and Courgettes with Charred Red Bell Peppers

Patlıcan-Kabak-Biber Kızartma

Ingredients

Red bell peppers	4
Cooking oil for frying	
Courgettes (zucchinis)	4, cut into 0.5-cm slices
Aubergines (eggplants)	4

Sauce

Extra virgin olive oil	4 Tbsp
Onion	1, medium, peeled and thinly sliced
Granulated sugar	1 tsp
Garlic	4 cloves, peeled and coarsely chopped
Green peppers	5, small, thinly sliced
Tomatoes	2, large, peeled and cut into cubes
Salt and ground black pepper	
Parsley	1/2 bunch, chopped

Method

- Prepare the sauce. Put the olive oil in a saucepan over medium heat. Add the onion and the sugar and let it caramelise a little. Add the garlic, green peppers and tomatoes. Season with salt and pepper. Cover and cook until tender. Add the parsley just before removing the pan from the heat. Set aside and let it cool.
- Place the red bell peppers over a flame and char them. Peel and remove the seeds.
- Put a generous amount of oil into a pan and fry the courgettes. Remove to a paper towel to drain.
- Peel the aubergines and cut into crosswise slices 0.5-cm thick. To avoid discolouring, fry them immediately in the same pan as the courgettes. Remove and drain well on paper towels.
- To serve, place a slice of aubergine on the plate, top with a piece of charred red bell pepper and then a slice of courgette. Repeat the layering process two more times and spoon the sauce over.

Imam Bayıldı (Stuffed Aubergines)
(Serves 4)

Ingredients

Vegetable oil for frying	
Aubergines (eggplants)	4, small, peeled
Extra virgin olive oil	2 Tbsp
Onions	2, medium, peeled and sliced
Granulated sugar	1 Tbsp
Garlic	4 cloves, peeled and thinly sliced
Tomatoes	2, peeled and cut into cubes
Green peppers	4, chopped
Salt	
Parsley	1 bunch, chopped

Method

- Put sufficient amount of oil into a frying pan (skillet) or use a deep-fryer. Fry the aubergines until they turn golden brown. Drain on paper towels.
- In a sauté pan, heat the olive oil and add the onions and granulated sugar. Cook until they slightly caramelise. Add the garlic, tomatoes and green peppers. Add salt and cook over low heat until the stuffing is tender.
- Remove from the heat and add the parsley. Adjust the seasoning and add pepper if desired.
- Slit the aubergines lengthwise and sprinkle salt inside. Fill with the stuffing and arrange the stuffed eggplants in a shallow pan. Add 2 Tbsp of hot water and cook for another 10 minutes over low heat. Serve warm or cold, as an appetiser or after the main course.

Pastry with Aubergine Filling
Patlıcanlı Poğaça

(Makes approximately 20 pieces)

Ingredients

Butter	110 g, melted
Vegetable oil	125 ml
Yoghurt	250 ml
Egg white	1
Salt	$^1/_2$ tsp
Baking soda	1 tsp
Plain (all-purpose) flour	500 g
Sesame seeds	

Filling

Olive oil	1 Tbsp
Ground (minced) beef	200 g
Salt and ground black pepper	
Onion	1, medium, peeled and cut into cubes
Green bell pepper	1, cored and thinly sliced
Red bell pepper	1, cored and thinly sliced
Aubergines (eggplants)	2
Egg yolk	1, beaten

Method

- First prepare the filling. Put the olive oil in a pan, add the ground beef and set on medium heat, stirring to avoid big lumps of meat. Season with salt and pepper. Add the onion and bell peppers. Cook on medium-low heat.
- Peel the aubergines, halve them and then cut into 1–1.5-cm cubes. Keep them in salted water as you proceed to avoid discolouring. When all done, strain, then rinse and transfer them to the pan. Adjust seasoning and cook for 10–12 minutes until all ingredients are well cooked and the filling is dry. Cool to room temperature.
- Set the oven to 175°C.
- Pour the melted butter and vegetable oil into a mixing bowl. Add the yoghurt and mix with a fork. Mix in the egg white, then the salt and baking soda. Mix well. Pour in most of the flour and stir with the fork. Then using your hands, start feeling the dough and add the rest of the flour until it becomes a soft dough with body. If you add too much flour, it will be easier to manage but the pastry will not be as crisp.
- Portion the dough with your hands. Shape each portion with the palm of your hands and flatten it. Put one spoonful of filling on each dough piece and bring together the ends, just as you would a dumpling. Shape into a crescent or rectangle and arrange on a tray. When all are done, brush the pastries with egg yolk. Sprinkle sesame seeds on top and transfer them into the oven. Bake for about 20 minutes until well-risen and golden brown in colour. Turn off the heat and keep the pastry in the oven for a further 5 minutes before serving.

POMEGRANATES *Nar*

Çarşıdan aldım bir tane (I bought one from the market)
Eve geldim bin tane (I came home and the one became a thousand)

This is a popular riddle, the answer to which is the pomegranate, that most exotic of summer fruits mentioned in various historical and mythological sources. Native to Iran, pomegranates were widely known in the ancient Mediterranean world, including the southern coasts of Turkey. Archival records also testify to the existence of pomegranate orchards around the Marmara Sea, the fertile hinterland of Istanbul. During the Ottoman Empire, the best and choicest fresh produce arriving in Istanbul was sold to the palace first and only then to the rest of the population. In his archival history of everyday life in Istanbul, Ahmet Refik documents an imperial decree from 1753 banning the harvesting from pomegranate orchards in Gemlik (on the southern shores of the Marmara Sea) before the best pomegranates were picked for the sultan's consumption.[3]

Today, pomegranates maintain a distinguished place in Turkish culinary culture and different varieties serve different purposes. Pomegranates with larger, pinkish and sweeter 'seeds' are eaten fresh or used as a decorative accent over some desserts, while those with smaller seeds and darker red juice are often squeezed to make a refreshing beverage, available at most snack kiosks or from an occasional street seller when pomegranates are in season. The most special use of the fruit however is for *nar ekşisi* (a kind of pomegranate vinegar) that gives a distinct southeastern flavour to many dishes from salads to *çiğ köfte* (raw meat and bulgur patties) (recipe on page 122).

Çarşıdan aldım bir tane
Eve geldim bin tane

I bought one from the market
I came home and the one became a thousand

Pomegranate trees, Antalya

From top A watermelon cart, Urfa; Famous Diyarbakır watermelons

Watermelon and melon truck, Istanbul

WATERMELONS *Karpuz*

The appearance of watermelons in grocery stores and street carts
is an unmistakable sign of summer everywhere. This glorious and
thirst-quenching fruit enjoys wide popularity in every part of
Turkey and across the entire social spectrum, from being common
menu items in the fanciest restaurants to providing a cheap and
refreshing accompaniment to packed homemade lunches of bread
and cheese. Although watermelons are grown across a wide
region of central and southern Anatolia, the southeastern city of
Diyarbakır distinguishes itself as the "Watermelon capital"
of Turkey. Diyarbakır watermelons are huge, elongated and sweet,
making "Diyarbakır" a sought-after name in watermelons.

Watermelon seeds, Adana

WATERMELON SEEDS *Karpuz Çekirdeği*

Visitors to Adana in southern Turkey are fascinated by carts of watermelon seeds that are characteristic fixtures of street life in the summer. For many Turks, these carts bring back memories of childhood when eating watermelon and sunflower seeds was an inseparable part of the experience of going to an open-air cinema on hot summer nights. In those years, they used to be home-prepared watermelon seeds: after eating watermelons, the seeds were collected and left to dry for subsequent consumption as a snack. Over time, imported watermelons with smaller seeds arrived, then the seedless ones followed, perhaps making the preparation of fruit salads easier, but taking away the fun of collecting and drying watermelon seeds. In recent years, the trend is thankfully reversed. Large "Diyarbakır watermelons" are once again filling carts and counters everywhere. Their large

seeds are also sold as a popular item in the streets. In Adana, sellers of watermelon seeds explain that the seeds are lightly soaked in boiling water, then drained, salted and air dried.

SUNFLOWER SEEDS *Ayçekirdeği*

Sunflower seeds are heaped on the three-wheeled cart parked in a side street leading to a fresh produce market in Ankara. People buy the small quantities that Mehmet, the young seller carefully weighs and puts in paper bags stacked in one corner. He explains that he brings his sunflower seeds from his uncle's fields in Kırıkkale to the north of Ankara and depending on the day of the week, he parks his cart near different neighbourhood markets. He sells fresh seeds, straight out of the flower. They are fuller, probably tastier and definitely healthier than the salted, roasted and pre-packaged kind that are available in grocery stores.

Sunflower seeds, Gaziantep

HAZELNUTS *Fındık*

Native to the Black Sea region, hazelnuts are the pride of the entire country since Turkey is the largest hazelnut producer in the world, followed by Italy and Spain.[4] Used extensively for cakes, cookies, chocolates, sweets and the exquisite hazelnut spread (the Turkish counterpart of peanut butter), they are also consumed as popular snacks along with pistachios and other nuts. In fact, they make highly prestigious and precious snacks "worthy of beautiful brunette women" as a popular Black Sea song goes: *"Ben esmeri fındık ile beslerim"* ("I feed my brunette with hazelnuts"). Of the two major varieties, it is the round, fat hazelnuts of the eastern Black Sea region that are roasted plain, salted or spiced in ovens or stove tops for consumption as a snack. The thinner, longer and more pointed varieties grown in the Değirmendere region of the western Black Sea coast are primarily for eating fresh. Piles of them appear in street carts by midsummer. Sometimes they are sold just as they were picked from the tree, in their brown shells, which in turn, are hidden snugly inside the green leaves called *çotanak*. More often, the sellers perform the first step and remove the shells from the leaves. They are then sold in small quantities for immediate consumption. Cracking the shells by pressing two of these hazelnuts together, eating the fresh meat inside and repeating the process with two more hazelnuts is a popular ritual of summer afternoons. In addition to these two major varieties, there is also a kind of edible wild hazelnut *(yabani fındık)* that grows by the small streams and creeks of northern Anatolia.[5]

From top Fresh hazelnuts for promenading crowds, Ayvalık; A close up view

Hazelnut Cookies *Fındıklı Kurabiye*

(Makes 25–30 mini cookies)

Ingredients

Margarine	150 g, softened
Plain (all-purpose) flour	300 g
Ground hazelnuts	90 g
Egg	1
Icing (confectioner's) sugar	5 Tbsp
Vanilla essence (extract)	$\frac{1}{2}$ tsp
Egg white	1
Hazelnuts	25–30, roasted

Method

- Combine the softened margarine with the flour in a mixer at slow speed or by hand until well incorporated. Add the ground hazelnuts, egg, icing sugar and vanilla essence. Mix and form into a dough.
- If using a cookie press, roll the dough on a floured surface and press into the tube. If shaping by hand, roll the dough out on a well-floured surface to 0.5-cm thickness. Cut out the desired shapes using a glass or cookie cutters. Whisk the egg white in a bowl and dip the cookies into the egg white. Arrange on a baking tray then place a hazelnut on top of each cookie. Bake in a preheated oven at 150°C for about 15 minutes or until lightly brown.

Unripe pistachios; outer skins still green, near Halfeti

PISTACHIOS *Şam Fıstığı* or *Antep Fıstığı*

Some of the tastiest pistachios in the world are grown in southeastern Turkey and beyond the Syrian border, hence the names *Antep Fıstığı* (Gaziantep Pistachio) and *Şam Fıstığı* (Damascus Pistachio). Pistachios constitute a major export item from the region although the rising waters of the dams over the Tigris and Euphrates rivers have flooded many pistachio trees, depriving many pistachio farmers of their traditional livelihood.

Roasted and salted pistachios are a favourite snack of many. They are also a tasty accompaniment with any drink while raw and unsalted pistachios are used extensively in regional dishes, as well as in desserts, cakes and ice cream everywhere across the country. Candied pistachio paste *(fıstık ezmesi)*, akin to the texture of marzipan, is another regional specialty that has spread all the way to Istanbul. It is an exquisite sweet, an elegant gift or treat that can be found in the fanciest confectioneries of Istanbul, like the centuries old Hacı Bekir or Cemilzade. The premium value attributed to pistachios is reflected in the Turkish language. For example, in reference to a beautiful young woman (or to anything admirable) it is common to use the expression: *Fıstık gibi maşallah!* ("She is like a pistachio, God protect her!")

A colourful snack, ripe pistachios with outer skins, Gaziantep

Pistachio coffee, downtown Gaziantep

Pistachio Coffee *Menengiç Kahvesi*

The most unusual pistachio product unique to southeastern
Turkey is pistachio coffee *(menengiç kahvesi)*. The *menengiç* plant
is a kind of wild pistachio that grows around Gaziantep. Its fruits
are picked when still small, then roasted, finely ground and
cooked just like Turkish coffee. Sold in brass pots carried by the
menengiç sellers of Gaziantep's busy market, this coffee has
a very different and unusual taste. It is sweet and sour,
reminiscent of the fresh pistachio pods. Drinkers of *menengiç*
kahvesi can see a thin film of oil on the surface of the coffee,
but this does not mean that it is a heavy beverage.

Menengiç *kahvesi* used to be served in small cups in the
same way that *mırra* (another special southeastern coffee,
see page 181) is served in the region, but nowadays, hygiene
concerns have necessitated a switch to disposable plastic cups.
This has taken away the traditional aesthetics of the *menengiç*
ritual but nonetheless, to come across the shiny *menengiç* pot
in the midst of the busy market is a nice surprise and a welcome
occasion for a short coffee break.

ÇIĞ KÖFTE (Raw Meat and Bulgur Patties)

Another famous specialty of the southeast, *çiğ köfte* is an
exception to the Turkish aversion to raw meat. Making *çiğ köfte*
is a long and laborious process in which the raw ground meat
is kneaded for a long time with fine bulgur and various spices,
especially the hot processed paprika *(isot)* specific to the region.
Since considerable strength is needed for this process, it is not
surprising that the makers/sellers of *çiğ köfte* are almost
exclusively men. A curious way of testing whether the meat has
been kneaded to perfection or not is by throwing it against a wall
(not unlike the way some people would test if spaghetti
is adequately cooked or not). If it sticks, it means that the
çiğ köfte is ready; if not, some more kneading is necessary.
When it is ready, *çiğ köfte* is usually served with sliced onions
and parsley topped with pomegranate vinegar *(nar ekşisi)*,
often with an accompanying glass of cold *ayran*. In recent years,
as a result of massive migration from the southeast, *çiğ köfte*
has entered restaurant menus in Istanbul and has become
a popular *meze* for *rakı* drinking—a development for which the
older and more refined Istanbulites have nothing but contempt.

Çiğ köfte for lunch, a busy main street in Adana

AYRAN (Yoghurt Drink)

Prepared by mixing yoghurt, water and salt, *ayran* is a very popular and heavily consumed beverage all over Turkey. It is especially effective in very hot weather, compensating the loss of salt from the body as a result of perspiration.

Sadık Usta is an *ayran* seller in Antakya, a cosmopolitan city of southern Turkey close to the Syrian border. He learned his trade from his father and has been in the business for 44 years. He remembers having started as a child, fetching water for his father. His own son, now drafted into the military, is also an *ayran* seller who helps out with a separate cart. Sadık Usta dreams of retirement as soon as his son returns from military service to take over the business. All these years, Sadık Usta has always carefully prepared his own *ayran*. He says that he looks at his customer's face to judge the quality of his *ayran*. Once, he detected a frown on a customer's face, followed by another frown on another customer's face a few minutes later. He then took a sip of *ayran* himself and realised that the cow that gave the milk for his yoghurt had been feeding on spring onions (scallions)! He explains that whatever the cows eat passes onto the smell of the milk and from there, to the yoghurt.

It is a delight to watch Sadık Usta serve his *ayran*. After rinsing the glass, he dips his *cezve* (a long-handled small pot typically for making Turkish coffee) into the *ayran*, ladles a generous amount into the glass and sprinkles it with as much salt as the customer desires. He then pours it back into the *cezve* and immediately returns it to the glass, repeating the procedure a few times to dissolve the salt.

His cart is packed with blocks of ice to keep his *ayran* cold for long hours. Still he prefers to "follow the shade" as he puts it. He meticulously plans where to park his cart during the morning hours and where to move it in the afternoon. This attention to detail is further seen in Sadık Usta's white shirt and cap which are always spotlessly clean. Such care and quality have earned him numerous customers who await his arrival every day, knowing exactly where he would be selling his *ayran* at a particular time of the day. In the early morning, Sadık Usta also sells *simit*, the popular sesame bagels that go well with *ayran* for a quick and cheap breakfast.

Sadık Usta serving *ayran* to his customers, Antakya

AUTUMN

In major Turkish cities, the trees change the colour of their leaves rather fast and without a dramatic display of autumn hues. It is thus the pumpkins, corn, apples, figs and late summer fruits and vegetables that give the season its characteristic colours.

In many parts of the country, the summer warmth lingers on well into October (or even November in the Mediterranean) and in some years, the Indian summer *(pastırma yazı)* can be as hot as midsummer. The intensity of street life picks up again in Istanbul, Ankara, Izmir and other major cities of Turkey, when people return from their summer houses and children start school in mid September. While wandering ice cream sellers disappear, others replace them bringing a rich variety of foods on their carts and trucks, from fresh produce, garlic and olives, to eggs and even live chickens. Some of the best summer fruits and vegetables can be purchased in early autumn and this is when women in traditional households set out to preserve and/or pickle them for winter consumption.

Figs of both green and purple varieties come out in late summer but attain their sweetest and ripest tastes in the early autumn. In late October, pumpkin carts appear in the streets and upon demand, the sellers cut and peel this quintessential autumn produce from which the ever-popular pumpkin dessert, *kabak tatlısı* is made. Unlike the pumpkin pie (that has become an icon of the American Thanksgiving), the Turks leave out the pie crust and instead make a syrupy dessert of cooked pumpkin slices, served with ground walnuts and clotted cream.

In major Turkish cities, the trees change the colour of their leaves rather fast and without a dramatic display of autumn hues. It is thus the pumpkins, corn, apples, figs and late summer fruits and vegetables that give the season its characteristic colours. Before long, the yellow leaves on the trees fall away in piles, leaving the branches naked and dreary. When the gusty winds start blowing colder and the days are noticeably shorter, winter is undoubtedly around the corner.

Opposite, clockwise from top left A feast to the eye; Red peppers; A young fig

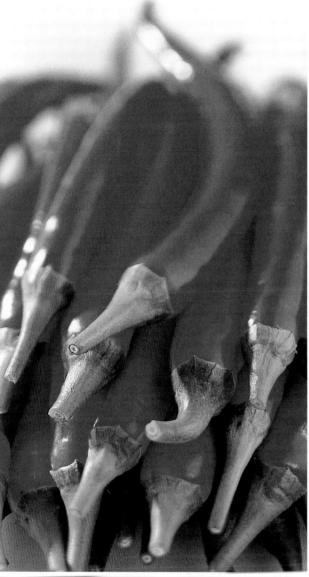

Grilled corn, Çanakkale

CORN *Mısır*

The most vivid images of corn in Turkish collective imaginary are those of the grilled and boiled varieties, sold on late summer or early autumn evenings in small hand-pushed carts lit by gas lamps. In the yellow glow of the gas lamps, these corn carts, decorated by beds of husks, create a magical atmosphere imprinted in many childhood memories. The seller of boiled corn wanders the streets yelling melodically, *"Süt mısır"* (literally "milk corn" or sweet corn) and when someone calls to him from a window or balcony above, he pulls his cart aside and stops. The customer comes down in a hurry, wallet in hand and inspects the corns in the large container after the seller lifts the lid. It is often difficult to decide. "This one!" she says and just when the selected corn is lifted with a pair of tongs, she says, "No, no that one is better!" After the final decision, the seller picks up the corn, carefully salts the whole cob and wraps it in a few green husks kept in a plastic bag for this purpose. The payment is made and he says, *"Afiyet olsun!"* ("Enjoy it!")

Others are addicts of grilled corn and they do not pay much attention to boiled corn carts. The sellers of grilled corn do not wander from street to street. They have their specific fixed locations where, using an old newspaper, they fan the fire of their small coal grills. When the ears of corns are thoroughly grilled, they are pulled to the side of the grill where they await their customers while still keeping warm. In recent years, another method has emerged—grilling the corn without removing the husks. After they are fully cooked, the husks are peeled and the corn is salted. Given the tastiness of the corn cooked this way, it is not surprising that it is proving to be increasingly popular.

There is also popcorn, which always adds to the pleasure of reclining in a movie theatre chair to watch a good film. And of course, we cannot forget corn bread, a traditional specialty of the Black Sea coast. As in many parts of the world, there are so many uses of this staple food. Brought from the New World and introduced to the rest of the world by Christopher Columbus, corn is an American icon. Almost half of the world's total corn is still produced in the Americas. It is believed that having reached Turkey via North Africa, Egypt and Syria, corn *(mısır)* was named after Egypt (also Mısır).

A cornfield, Muğla

Corn Bread *Mısır Ekmeği*
(Makes 1 loaf)

Ingredients

Corn flour (cornstarch)	500 g
Warm water	500 ml
Yoghurt	1 Tbsp
Baking soda	1 tsp
Salt	¼ tsp
Granulated sugar	1 tsp

Method

- Mix the corn flour and warm water. The mixture should have the consistency of a pudding. Add the yoghurt, baking soda, salt and sugar. Mix well.
- Let the mixture stand at room temperature for 15 minutes, then turn it into a well-greased or non-stick loaf tin. Bake at 200°C in a preheated oven for 35–40 minutes, until the top is slightly brown. Let it cool in the tin for 10 minutes, then remove and slice. As a variation to this recipe, you can also add corn kernels or thinly sliced sun-dried tomatoes into the mixture during the final step of mixing,

Polenta with Jumbo Prawns and Spicy Tomato Sauce

Mısır Pelteli Jumbo Karides
(Serves 4)

Ingredients

Polenta

Water	625 ml
Milk	125 ml
Salt	
Corn flour (cornstarch)	125 g

Sauce

Vegetable oil	1 Tbsp
Grated ginger	1 Tbsp
Garlic	4 cloves, peeled and sliced
Yellow, red and green bell peppers	1 each, cored and cut into 3-mm thick slices
Tomatoes	3, peeled, seeded and coarsely chopped
Ground white pepper	
Parsley	1 bunch, chopped
Chilli powder	1 tsp
Butter	1 tsp
Jumbo prawns (shrimps)	12, cleaned, deveined and shelled with tails intact

Method

- Prepare the polenta. Bring the water and milk to the boil and add some salt. While the liquid is boiling, add the corn flour and stir with a whisk. Reduce the heat and cook for 10 minutes, stirring continuously to avoid lumps. Pour the polenta into a wide, shallow container and let it cool. It should ideally be about 1-cm deep.
- Heat the oil in a pan then sauté the ginger and garlic briefly. Add the bell peppers and sauté for 5 minutes until they start to get tender. Add the tomatoes, season with salt and pepper and cook covered for a further 5 minutes. When ready, sprinkle with parsley and chilli powder and keep covered until serving.
- Season the prawns with salt and pepper. Heat the grill for the prawns. If the grill is not non-stick, add a little oil before placing the prawns on. Grill for about 3 minutes on each side until well cooked, with grill marks.
- Cut the polenta with a ring cutter or with the rim of a glass tumbler. In a small pan, add the butter and heat the polenta discs, about 2 minutes each side. Place a polenta disc on a serving plate, pour enough sauce to cover it and arrange three prawns around the polenta to serve.

A pumpkin seller removing the hard skins of the pumpkins, Kadıköy, Istanbul

PUMPKINS *Balkabağı*

Huge and tough-skinned, pumpkins are a formidable challenge for the aspiring cook, but once the difficulty of cutting and peeling are overcome, it is a rewarding fruit. When pumpkins are in season, many street sellers offer the extra help of cutting the pumpkins and removing the hard skins for their customers. The most traditional and popular use of pumpkin in Turkish cuisine is the delightful pumpkin dessert *(kabak tatlısı)*—simple slices of pumpkin cooked with sugar until soft and syrupy, then served with ground walnuts and/or clotted cream. To those who do not think very highly of the pumpkin, the transformation of this rough and rather ordinary fruit into an exquisite dessert may seem as amazing as the transformation of Cindrella's pumpkin into an elegant carriage. Pumpkins belong to the *kabak* family,

a generic word that includes courgette (zucchini) and squash as well, although the latter are often specified as "green" or "fresh" *(yeşil kabak, taze kabak)*, reserving the word *kabak* exclusively for the pumpkin. However, Turkish popular parlance is not very kind to the pumpkin. A tasteless melon is said to be *kabak gibi* ("like a pumpkin") and a shiny bald head is a *kabak kafa* ("pumpkin head"). As for the seeds of the pumpkin, commercially dried, salted and roasted, they make a very popular and cheap snack sold by the kilogram. As testimony to the population's passion for pumpkin and sunflower seeds, one can spot piles of empty shells in every public space, from the streets, sidewalks, urban squares and stadiums, to the open air cinemas.

Pumpkin Soup *Balkabağı Çorbası*
(Serves 4)

Ingredients

Pumpkin	500 g, skinned and seeded
Milk	200 ml
Grated ginger	1 Tbsp
Ground nutmeg	a pinch
Garlic	5 cloves, peeled
Beef stock or court bouillon	750 ml
Salt and ground white pepper	
Light cream	

Method

- Clean the pumpkin well, then cut into cubes, removing any hard or green parts. Steam the pumpkin cubes for 5 minutes until tender. Remove to a plate and reserve the steaming liquid.
- In a pot, combine the milk, grated ginger, ground nutmeg and garlic cloves and bring to the boil. Add the pumpkin and stir for a few minutes with a wooden spoon until the mixture becomes a thick lumpy purée. Transfer to a blender and blend well until smooth. If it is too dense to mix, add some of the steaming liquid to help. Return the purée to the pot and add the beef stock or court bouillon, salt and pepper and bring to the boil. Adjust the seasoning and simmer for a few minutes.
- Spoon the soup into individual serving bowls and with the help of a squeeze bottle or a spoon, drizzle light cream over before serving.

Pumpkin Pie *Balkabaklı Turta*

(Serves 8)

Ingredients

Pastry Shell

Plain (all-purpose) flour	200 g
Salt	½ tsp
Cold butter	100 g, cut into cubes
Egg	1
Cold water	1–2 Tbsp, if needed

Pumpkin Filling

Pumpkin	500 g, shelled and seeded
Brown sugar	100 g
Cinnamon sticks	2
Cloves	a few
Ground ginger	½ tsp
Eggs	2
Milk	350 ml
Heavy cream	50 ml

Method

- Sift the flour and salt onto the work surface. Work the butter in with your hands until it looks sandy in texture. Form it into a mound and make a well in the centre. Whisk the egg and pour into the well. Incorporate the flour and egg with your hands but do not overwork. Add cold water if the mixture is too dry.
- Take small pieces from the dough and press on the work surface with the palm of your hand, making a smooth dough. Bring the pieces together and form into a ball. Cover and keep refrigerated for 20 minutes.
- Roll the chilled and rested dough out onto a floured surface and place into a tart shell 25 cm in diameter. Remove excess flour with a brush.
- Cut the pumpkin into small pieces and place in a shallow pan. Sprinkle the brown sugar on, add the cinnamon sticks, cloves and ground ginger and cook over medium heat for 15–20 minutes until the pumpkin is tender. Remove the cinnamon sticks and cloves and drain the liquid. Mash the pumpkin with a fork.
- In a deep bowl, mix the eggs, milk, heavy cream and pumpkin purée. Adjust the flavour by adding ground cinnamon, ground cloves and ground ginger, if necessary.
- Preheat the oven to 170°C. Pour the filling into the tart shell and bake for 40 minutes until the top is slightly brown. Let the pie rest for about 1 hour before slicing. Serve with ice cream or whipped cream.

Crêpes with Pumpkin Purée *Balkabaklı Krep*
(Serves 4)

Ingredients

Pumpkin	400 g, skinned and seeded
Granulated sugar	200 g
Cinnamon sticks	2
Cloves	a few
Water	125 ml
Plain (all-purpose) flour	3 Tbsp
Milk	600 ml
Vanilla essence (extract)	½ tsp
Eggs	4
Chocolate or hazelnut spread (optional)	

Garnish
Chocolate shavings
Icing (confectioner's) sugar
Ground cinnamon

Method

- Cut the pumpkin into small cubes and place in a shallow pan. Sprinkle sugar on top, then add cinnamon sticks, cloves and water. Cover and let it cook until soft. Remove cinnamon sticks and cloves and transfer to a bowl. Mash the pumpkin with the back of a fork. Set aside.

- In another bowl, mix the flour with a few tablespoons of milk and avoid forming any lumps. Add vanilla essence and then the eggs one at a time. Mix well. (Using a whisk will create foam so you may want to use a fork.) Finally add the rest of the milk and let it stand in the refrigerator for 30 minutes.

- Heat a non-stick frying pan (skillet) over medium heat. Pour a small amount of the mixture onto the hot pan and spread it out to make a crêpe. Cook each side for about 1 minute and transfer to a plate. Repeat until the mixture is used up. Stack the crêpes on top of one another. The number of crepes will depend on the size of the frying pan.

- Place a crêpe on a serving plate. Top with a spoonful of pumpkin purée and spread well. Sandwich with another crepe and spread with a spoonful of hazelnut or chocolate spread. (Alternatively, use only pumpkin puree in all layers.) Repeat 4–5 times to make a layered "crêpe cake". You may use whole crepes to make a large cake or a cookie cutter to make small crêpe cakes for individual servings. Sprinkle with chocolate shavings and/or icing sugar and ground cinnamon.

Figs on display along the Bosphorus, Istanbul

FIGS *Incir*

Question: What is a fig leaf between two stones?

Answer: Adam ironing his pants.

Jokes and riddles of this sort abound in every culture, along with the metaphorical use of the fig leaf for a face-saving cover up. Whether or not the fig leaf was indeed the original clothing of Adam and Eve, there is no doubt that fig trees are among the oldest species known in human history. Mentioned in all three monotheistic religions originating in the eastern Mediterranean basin, the fig is one of two iconic Mediterranean fruit, the other being the olive. With its distinct smell, texture and form, the fig tree is a characteristic element of the rugged Mediterranean landscape. Its delicious fruit is consumed extensively in Turkey: fresh when in season, and in jams, cakes and sweets throughout the year. Dried figs are also among the country's major exports.

After peeling a ripe fig, cut it in half and before eating, contemplate the amazing cross section with the hundreds of tiny seeds—one of the great wonders of mother nature. The tininess of these seeds has even entered the Turkish language in the form of a common idiom: when a particular matter or conversation is unimportant or insignificant, people say: *"Incir çekirdeğini doldurmaz!"* ("It wouldn't fill a fig seed!")

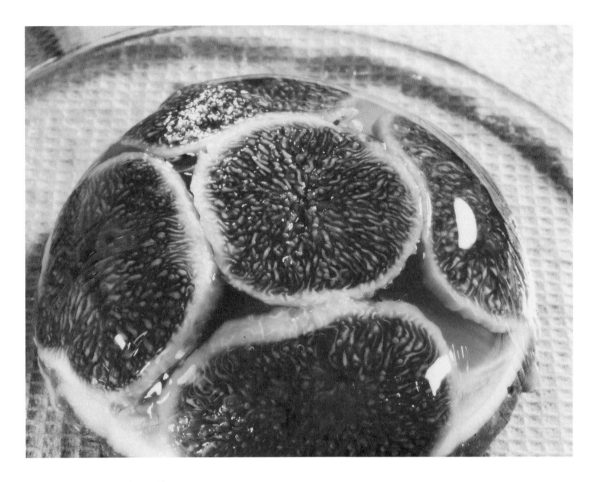

Jelly with Figs *Incirli Jöle*
(Serves 4)

Ingredients

Figs	7–8, medium, peeled and cut into 0.3-cm thick slices
Jelly powder (plain)	500 ml
Yoghurt	6 Tbsp
Petit beurre or plain	
tea biscuits	150 g, roughly broken
Chocolate chips	2 Tbsp

Method

- Use figs with good texture and colour. Line individual bowls with cling film (plastic wrap) and arrange the slices of fig to plaster the inside of the bowl.
- Prepare the jelly according to the instructions on the pack. Divide it into three equal portions. Pour one portion over the sliced figs right away and put the bowls into the refrigerator to set. Pour the other two portions into two deep bowls. Pour the yoghurt into one of these bowls and mix well with a spoon. Take the bowls with the figs and set jelly out of the refrigerator and pour the jelly-yoghurt mixture equally into the bowls. Return the bowls to the refrigerator for the second layer to set.
- Put the broken biscuits into the third portion of jelly and mix. When it is cool enough not to melt the chocolate, add the chocolate chips. Top the bowls in the refrigerator with this final layer and chill to set completely. This is a very easy dessert to prepare but it takes about 2 hours to set. It is important not to rush this as layers may get mixed.
- Turn bowls upside down and pop jelly out onto serving plates. Remove cling film and serve.

Fig Jam *Incir Reçeli*

In the right season, it is very typical in Turkey to buy fresh figs for jam, already peeled and ready to cook. These special "jam figs" are small green figs which are picked earlier than the regular fresh figs. If you do not have this luxury of buying "jam figs", it is important to peel the figs first. Among the different varieties of fruit jam, fig jam is probably the one with shortest shelf life, as it crystallises more quickly than the other varieties.

Ingredients

Figs	1 kg, peeled
Granulated sugar	1 kg
Ground cinnamon	$^1/_2$ tsp or 2 cinnamon sticks

Method

- Put the figs in a pot and cover with water. Bring to the boil and cook for 10 minutes until the figs are slightly tender. Drain well and leave to cool. When the figs are cool enough to handle, squeeze well with your hands. This procedure takes away the bitter taste of the figs.
- Put the figs into another pot, add sugar and cook over low heat until it exudes its own juices. When there is enough liquid and it comes to a boil, let the figs simmer until soft, then remove them with a slotted spoon so they do not break or become mushy.
- Continue boiling the remaining liquid until it comes close to the desired consistency of jam. Return the figs to the pot. Add the cinnamon which enhances the flavour of the figs and simmer them all together for another 10 minutes. Remove from heat and let it cool. Store in jars.

Variety of olives, Urla, Izmir

OLIVES *Zeytin*

No other fruit carries as much symbolic and mythological significance as the olive, a fruit of the Mediterranean with more than 4,000 years of history behind it, much of which is still visible in the olive oil jars and amphorae of ancient civilisations recovered by archaeologists. Together with the fig tree (the "Tree of Truth"), the wild olive tree (the "Tree of Life") is mentioned in the sacred texts of the three major religions, and for centuries, it has been the source of much that has made the world a better place: oil for lamps, for cooking and for soaps. It is mentioned in the Koran as a sacred tree and many devout Muslims prefer to break their daily fast with a single black olive during the holy month of Ramadan. The olive branch (held by the white dove) is still a potent symbol of peace in today's chaotic world.

Sturdy and resistant to draughts, olive trees grow in vast areas along the Aegean coast and the Marmara region, Ayvalık and Gemlik being the two major centres respectively. Sold in cheap plastic containers in the streets and neighbourhood markets of Turkish cities, olives of both black and green varieties are standard items on breakfast tables across the social spectrum. The presentation of olives is an art form in itself: the green ones with slices of lemon, the black ones dressed with lemon juice and olive oil and sprinkled with oregano and crushed paprika. Black olive paste sold in jars or plastic tubes is another Turkish specialty that makes a tasty spread on bread or crackers.

In terms of the number of olive trees and the production of olives and olive oil, Turkey ranks among the top five countries in the world.[1] Traditionally, the consumption of olive oil was relatively low for a Mediterranean country (most of the cooking was done with butter, margarine or other vegetable oils), but in recent years, the gourmet potential of fine olive oils has been rediscovered. Extra virgin olive oils are increasingly more available and varied in boutique food stores, and also more appreciated in gourmet cooking and dining. (The classification "extra virgin" indicates a low acidity of less than one per cent, a very desirable property for flavour.[2])

Peppers drying in the sun, Izmir

RED PEPPERS *Kırmızı Biber*

Although the large and fat red bell peppers are rare in Turkey, a longer and thinner variety appears in the streets and the fresh produce markets of major cities in early summer and becomes abundantly available through the autumn. The most popular method of preparing red peppers is char-grilling or roasting them after which the outer skin peels off easily. Thus peeled and

simple but delicious appetisers. Sun-dried red peppers are also very common in Turkey, and they are used in numerous dishes when fresh ones are not available. A traditional way of drying red peppers is using a large needle and a sturdy string for threading them like a necklace and hanging this pepper 'necklace' in a place where it receives direct sunlight.

Char-Grilled Red Pepper Soup *Közlenmiş Kırmızı Biber Çorbası*
(Serves 4)

Ingredients

Red peppers	7, long and thin
Butter	1 Tbsp
Onion	1, peeled and sliced
Garlic	3 cloves, peeled and crushed
Fennel bulb	1, sliced into thin rounds
Tomatoes	2, peeled, seeded and coarsely chopped
Celery	1, small, peeled and chopped in chunks
Green bell peppers	2, cored and sliced
Red pepper paste	1 Tbsp
Hot water	1 litre
Salt and ground white pepper	

Method

- Place the red peppers over the flame of the stove. Char them turning continuously until they have many black spots. Put them into a bowl, cover with cling film (plastic wrap) and let them stand for 5 minutes. Peel the skin, remove the seeds and chop coarsely.

- In a pot, add the butter and onion and start cooking over medium heat until the onion starts to soften. Add garlic, fennel, tomatoes, celery and bell peppers one after the other and cook over low heat for 15 minutes until all the flavours are exuded and vegetables are soft.

- Add the red pepper paste and hot water and bring to the boil. Add salt and ground white pepper and let it simmer for 20 minutes. Then purée well using a blender. Adjust seasoning and return to the pot for serving.

Fillet on Red Bell Pepper Sauce
Biber Soslu Bonfile
(Serves 4)

Ingredients

Sauce

Olive oil	2 Tbsp
Onion	1, small, peeled and coarsely chopped
Red bell peppers	4, cored, seeded and cut into even pieces
Tomatoes	2, peeled and chopped
Salt and ground white pepper	
Tomato paste	1 Tbsp
Bay leaves	2
Garlic	3 cloves, peeled and crushed
Vegetable oil	2 Tbsp
Spinach	1 bunch, hard stems removed
Butter	1 Tbsp
Beef fillet (tender cut)	4 pieces

Method

- Put the olive oil in a pan and add the onion. Start cooking on low heat. Add bell peppers and cook for 5 minutes until they soften.
- Add tomatoes, salt, pepper, tomato paste and bay leaves. Add garlic, then cover and cook for about 30 minutes. If the tomatoes are not the juicy type, you may need to add a little water or tomato juice. When done, discard the bay leaves and purée the mixture in the blender. Adjust the seasoning.
- Reheat the pan with half the vegetable oil. Add the spinach and sprinkle salt and pepper. Cook for 1 minute until wilted. Set aside.
- In the same pan over high heat, add the remaining vegetable oil and butter. Season the beef with salt and pepper and place into the sizzling pan. After 30 seconds, shake the pan and flip beef fillet. Sear the beef fillet over high heat and cook according to taste. Serve over red bell pepper sauce and wilted spinach.

Garlic heads, Istanbul

GARLIC *Sarımsak*

Like its cousin the onion, garlic is used widely, from appetisers and pickles to olive oil dishes and yoghurt sauces. Although complaints about its strong smell are always there, it is impossible to imagine Turkish cuisine without garlic. To deal with the smell, cloves, mints or other breath-cleaning herbs and candies are often offered after a garlic-based meal both in restaurants and homes. Locally grown garlic typically has smaller bulbs, whereas the imported varieties are perfectly shaped and bigger, with three to four times more cloves than the local ones.

For such a humble and common root vegetable, garlic has a surprisingly prominent place in folk mythology. For many superstitious Turks, the belief in its supernatural powers to ward off all kinds of evil are as significant as its culinary and nutritious potential. As with many other cultures, braids of garlic hanging by the door are believed to protect the home from evil spirits. Small porcelain bulbs of garlic, along with the "evil eye" and blue beads are characteristic motifs of Turkish popular culture, hanging from doors and car mirrors, worn as bracelets or used as charms on key holders.

A young farmer selling garlic in the streets of Beykoz on the Asian side of Istanbul explains that he grows the garlic in his own fields in Kastamonu in central Anatolia. He and his family harvest it themselves and he drives a truckload to Istanbul in September each year to sell in the streets of different neighbourhoods. Here is another example of a livelihood earned by selling a single item—heaps of plump, fresh garlic heads!

Fresh garlic, Muğla

Fresh almond seller, Istanbul

ALMONDS ON ICE *Buzlu Badem*

In one of the busiest corners of Nişantaşı, an upper class district of Istanbul, one can find Murtaza who sells fresh almonds piled on a block of ice on a cart. The ice keeps the almonds cool and always moist. With a flip of the finger, the outer skin comes off easily, revealing the fresh almond. The taste of Murtaza's almonds are heavenly. They come from the almond orchards of Çanakkale, some 300 kilometres west of Istanbul at the tip of the straits of the Dardanelles. Murtaza reveals that he has customers from all over the city and he makes special deliveries to some of them. He gives out his cell phone number assuring everyone that his almonds are always only a telephone call away.

For such a relatively expensive snack, almonds on ice *(buzlu badem)* enjoy an unusually wide consumption in Turkey. Served on a bed of ice, fresh almonds always have a distinguished place on the table, especially when *rakı* drinking is in progress. From midsummer into autumn, itinerant almond sellers appear in and around the gardens or terraces of fish restaurants tempting the *rakı* drinkers with this refreshing compliment to their various appetisers. Although under no other circumstances do restaurants allow food from outside their own kitchens to be consumed on the premises, *buzlu badem* is an exception by consensus. Many restaurant diners purchase small amounts of almonds from the wandering sellers and the waiters do not object to serving them on restaurant plates when requested. It is as if all parties benefit from this ritual which prolongs and adds to the pleasure of eating and drinking in cheerful company.

KELLE Lamb Heads

For many visitors to Turkey, cooked lamb heads *(kelle)* staring at passers-by is a bizarre sight and probably not a particularly appetising one. But for most Turks, the head of the lamb is a delicacy reserved for special occasions. After the lamb is butchered and its meat and other parts utilised, the heads are roasted thoroughly in commercial ovens and sold in the streets or served in restaurants, always with a choice of "with" or "without the brain" *(beyinli* or *beyinsiz)*. Most people consider the meat from the cheeks of the lamb to be the tastiest. The tongue and the brain are also popular parts of the head. In most restaurants, these choice parts are served in thin slices, sprinkled with oregano and embellished with tomatoes and spring onions (scallions). The eyes, although included in the restaurant servings to give a sense of the entire head, are often discarded.

Kelle occupies an important place among the popular beliefs and collective imagination of the Turkish people. In the Kızıltepe and Ova villages of Mardin in southeastern Turkey, *kelle* is a special offering reserved only for guests of high status, prestige and respectability. The same tradition can be observed in Kazakistan (one of the Turkic republics of the former Soviet Union) where *kelle* is offered to the most important guest or to the leader of a community, following the motto: *Baş başa gider* ("The head goes to the head").[3] In contrast, a pregnant woman's cravings for *kelle* is considered an ominous sign, necessitating the sacrifice of a chicken to dispel any bad omens. Other interesting beliefs abound among the Turkomans of Iraq, Syria and Anatolia. For example in Keleki, it is customary to look at the ears of the lamb's head as a way of foretelling whether a pregnant woman will give birth to a boy or a girl—a fleshy ear predicts a baby girl, a bony one, a baby boy.[4] The most amusing usage of *kelle* in the Turkish language, however, is the expression: *pişmiş kelle gibi sırıtmak* ("grinning like a cooked lamb's head"), designating a silly and sleazy grin.

From top Almonds on ice, Nişantaşı, Istanbul; Heads for sale! Samanpazarı, Ankara

Itinerant egg seller, late 19th century (Istanbul Metropolitan Municipality, Atatürk Library) Putting all your eggs in one basket!

EGGS *Yumurta*

Crates or baskets of farm fresh eggs are other standard fixtures of neighbourhood markets and street commerce. Eggs are consumed in large quantities in Turkish cuisine (cholesterol-consciousness is a relatively recent phenomenon and still not pervasive), as omelettes, hardboiled eggs, sunny-side up over spinach *(ıspanaklı mıkla)* or with tomatoes and peppers *(menemen,* recipe on page 106). They are also primary ingredients of a wide range of dishes, soups and pastries, including the versatile mayonnaise that goes into everything, from sandwiches to Russian salad *(Rus salatası).* Introduced into the Turkish culinary culture by Russian *émigrés* fleeing the Bolshevik Revolution in 1917, *Rus salatası* is today a popular appetiser and side dish. No one knows exactly how the familiar Russian salad came to be called American salad at a certain point in history, but one can speculate that this new name corresponds to the politics of Cold War when Turkey became a staunch American ally. Unlike the Turkish-American strategic alliance however, the name of the appetiser has not stuck and most Turks still know it as the Russian salad.

RICE PILAF WITH CHICKPEAS
Nohutlu Pilav

History records that Mahmut Paşa, the grand vizier of Mehmed II (the conqueror of Istanbul in 1453), gave weekly banquets to palace bureaucrats, religious leaders, important military figures and other notables, and that rice with chickpeas constituted the traditional main course of these banquets. It is also noted that as a little game, he got his cooks to put chickpea-sized gold pieces in the rice and gave them to any guest who happened to pick them up in his spoon.[5]

Nowadays the rituals of rice with chickpeas are somewhat different. More than those who consume it during the day as a cheap lunch, it is the poorer night crowds that patronise the mobile glass cases in which this popular dish is sold. In the back streets of Beyoğlu, the heart of Istanbul's nightlife, long nights of heavy alcohol consumption end either in tripe soup restaurants *(işkembeci)* or, for those who cannot afford such a delicacy, a rice with chickpeas stand. Needless to say, rice with chickpeas is also standard fare in most Turkish households, as it is a basic but delicious dish to accompany meat and chicken.

Late night meal in the backstreets of Beyoğlu—rice pilaf with chickpeas

Rice Pilaf with Chickpeas *Nohutlu Pilav*
(Serves 4)

Ingredients

Chickpeas	100 g, soaked overnight
Rice	225 g
Butter or margarine	1 Tbsp
Chicken broth	500 ml
Salt and ground white pepper	

Method

- Drain the chickpeas and wash well. Transfer them to a pot, add some salt and cook until tender. Drain and set aside.
- Wash the rice to remove any starch. Rinse until the water runs clear.
- Melt the butter or margarine in a pot and add the rice. Cook until slightly browned then add the chicken broth, salt and pepper. Bring to the boil and then lower the heat. When most of the liquid is absorbed, add the drained chickpeas. Mix and lower the heat further. Cover and cook for about 10 minutes until all the liquid is absorbed. Serve with chicken or as a side dish.

Russian/American Salad *Rus/Amerikan Salatası*
(Serves 4)

Ingredients

Carrots	2, peeled and cut into pea-sized cubes
Potatoes	2, peeled and cut into pea-sized cubes
Fresh or frozen peas	150 g
Pickled cucumbers	150 g, sliced
Mayonnaise*	1 recipe

Mayonnaise

Egg yolk	1
Mustard	1 Tbsp
Salt and ground white pepper	
Vegetable oil	150 ml
Lemon juice	1 Tbsp

Method

- Prepare the mayonnaise. Put the egg yolk, mustard, salt and pepper into a bowl. Combine with an electric mixer. Add the oil in a steady and slow stream and incorporate totally. Add the lemon juice. Adjust seasoning.
- Steam the carrots, potatoes and peas separately until all are tender. Mix them and add the sliced pickles. Mix in the mayonnaise.

Börek with Spinach and Eggs *Ispanaklı ve Yumurtalı Börek*
(Serves 4)

Ingredients

Spinach	500 g, leaves plucked, stems discarded
Cooking oil	250 ml
Eggs	4
Salt and ground white pepper	
Chilli flakes	
Yoghurt	2 Tbsp
Filo pastry	2 sheets
Butter (optional)	1 Tbsp

Method

• Wash and dry the spinach leaves. Break into big pieces using your hands. Set them aside in a large bowl.

• In a frying pan (skillet), heat half the oil and add 3 eggs. Cook as you would scrambled eggs then remove from heat and pour over the spinach. Season with salt, pepper and chilli flakes. Mix well.

• In a small bowl, mix the rest of the oil, yoghurt and the remaining egg. Set aside.

• Place a filo sheet over the worktop. Put half of the yoghurt mixture over the sheet, specially working at the edges with your hands or with a pastry brush. Fold two opposite sides toward the middle, forming a thicker rectangle. Place the spinach in the middle and fold the sides in, forming a square. Transfer to a non-stick pan and cook over medium heat for about 4 minutes on each side until the pastry feels dry and moves with the pan when you shake it. When done, remove to a serving plate and spread the butter on, letting it melt with the heat of the pastry. Repeat the process for the other filo sheet.

• Allow the *börek* to cool a little before cutting. Garnish with roasted pine nuts as desired.

Courgette Fritters *Mücver*
(Serves 4)

Ingredients

Courgettes (zucchinis)	2, grated
Plain (all-purpose) flour	4 Tbsp
Salt	to taste
Freshly ground black pepper	to taste
Baking soda	$1/2$ tsp
Eggs	4
Milk	200 ml
Feta cheese	100 g, grated
Dill	$1/2$ bunch, chopped
Cooking oil	

Method

- Place the grated courgettes on a piece of cheesecloth. Squeeze to get rid of all the excess water. Transfer to a bowl, then add the flour, salt, freshly ground black pepper and baking soda. Mix well with a fork. Add the eggs, one after the other, avoiding lumps forming.
- Add the milk and mix well. Finally add the cheese and dill. Cover and let the mixture rest in the refrigerator for 10 minutes. If you are short of time, you may skip this part but this resting period helps the flour absorb the liquid better.
- Put a generous amount of oil in a frying pan (skillet). Heat it well but do not let it smoke. Using a spoon, drop equal amounts of the mixture into the sizzling pan. (An ice-cream scoop may help to make even-sized fritters.) Fry both sides and transfer them to a plate lined with paper towels to absorb excess oil. When ready, the fritters can be served with plain or garlic yoghurt according to taste. Garnish with sprigs of dill.

LIVE CHICKENS

Among all the street foods of Turkey, live chickens constitute
the greatest and most amusing surprise. It is also a rather noisy
reminder of how little things have changed since the time of the
wandering fowl sellers of the Ottoman period. Live chickens are
stacked into small cages in twos or threes and the cages are
stacked in rows, displayed for sale on small three-wheeled carts
(in Adana in the south) or open trucks (in Van in eastern Turkey).
The basic idea is not that different from a medieval peasant
holding a chicken under his arm to sell in the market. Yet, the
quantities are larger and the business is 'mobilised', a curious
combination of the old with the new! One cannot help thinking
about all the work that is needed before these pecking creatures
turn into, say, chicken kebabs! The thought is enough to make one
grateful for the commercially prepared chicken available on
supermarket shelves. Progress is not always for the worse!

Top Cartload of live chickens, Adana

Inset Itinerant fowl seller, late 19th century
(Istanbul Metropolitan Municipality, Atatürk
Library)

Grilled Chicken Skewers with Taboulé
Izgara Tavuk Şiş, Kısır Ile
(Serves 4)

Ingredients

Chicken breast	600 g, cut into 3-cm cubes
Salt and ground black pepper	
Extra virgin olive oil	3 Tbsp
Cherry tomatoes	
(red and yellow)	500 g
Rosemary	8 long stalks

Taboulé

Bulgur	250 g
Lemon juice	extracted from 3 lemons
Tomatoes	4, peeled, seeded and coarsely chopped
Garlic	4 cloves, peeled
Green bell pepper	1, cored and finely chopped
Red bell pepper	1, cored and finely chopped
Cucumbers	4, finely chopped
Parsley	1 bunch, finely chopped
Mint	4 bunches, finely chopped
Extra virgin olive oil	125 ml

Method

- Prepare the *taboulé*. Put the bulgur into a deep bowl, add lemon juice and tomatoes. Pass the garlic through a garlic press into the bowl and add the bell peppers, cucumbers, parsley and mint together with the olive oil, some salt and pepper. Let it stand at room temperature for 2 hours or overnight if refrigerated.
- Place the chicken cubes in a deep bowl, add salt, pepper and olive oil and keep refrigerated for 30 minutes.
- Meanwhile, remove the lower leaves of the rosemary. Use them to skewer the chicken pieces and cherry tomatoes. Sprinkle more salt and pepper to taste.
- Heat the grill. Place the skewers over the grill and let each side cook until there are grill marks and the chicken pieces are tender. Serve with *taboulé*.

Pan-fried Quail with Sweet and Sour Pilaf and Greens
Yeşillik ve Tahıllar Üzerinde Tavada Bıldırcın
(Serves 4)

Ingredients

Cannellini beans	100 g, soaked overnight
Chickpeas	100 g, soaked overnight
Barley	120 g, soaked overnight
Granulated sugar	110 g
Salt	to taste
Butter	4 Tbsp
Corn flour (cornstarch)	1 tsp
Balsamic vinegar	50 ml
Plums	8, cut in quarters and pitted
Lemon juice (optional)	extracted from 1 lemon
Filo pastry	2 sheets
Cooking oil	1 Tbsp
Ground black pepper	
Quails	4
Mixed greens	
Quail eggs	4, hardboiled and shelled

Method

- Wash the soaked beans, chickpeas and barley and cook in a pot with twice the amount of water as ingredients. When the water comes to the boil, add sugar and a pinch of salt. Let it simmer for about 1 hour until all are tender. Drain the excess water.
- In a pot, melt 1 Tbsp butter and add corn flour. Mix well into a paste. Add balsamic vinegar and when all is incorporated, add the plums. Cook for 10 minutes until the plums exude juices and become somewhat mushy. If the plums are ripe and very sweet, add some lemon juice. Remove from the heat and combine with the beans, chickpeas and barley. Mix them gently.
- Use either two individual tartlet moulds or two ovenproof dishes. Fold the filo sheets into 6 layers and place a mould in the middle. Cut around the mould with some reserve using the tip of a knife or a pair of scissors. Melt 2 Tbsp butter and grease the filo layers separately. Stack the layers on top of one another and place into the mould, pressing the other mould on top of it. Cook in a preheated oven at 170°C for 2–3 minutes. Watch carefully as it tends to burn easily. Remove the filo bowl from the mould; it should be firm, crisp and golden brown.
- Put remaining butter and oil into a frying pan (skillet) and heat well. Sprinkle salt and pepper over the quails and place in the pan, searing all sides well. Cover and cook for 5 minutes, turning the quails a couple of times. Cook until tender but crisp.
- Toss the greens with some lemon juice, salt and pepper. Put a generous amount on a serving plate. Place the filo bowl on the greens and fill with the beans, chickpeas and barley with plum sauce. Place quail on top and decorate with quail eggs.

Meyan sherbet sellers from different cities of southeastern Anatolia

Sack of sassafras roots, Gaziantep

***MEYAN* SHERBET** *Meyan Şerbeti*

Meyan sherbet is heavily consumed in southeastern Turkey, around Adana, Urfa and Gaziantep. The street sellers of this popular drink make music with the small metal bowls that they rhythmically hit against each other. After a while, the sound of these bowls becomes so familiar that one unconsciously registers the presence of a seller nearby at the slightest sound. The shiny brass containers that the sellers carry on their backs are ingeniously designed. After rinsing the glasses with water from a small tap attached to the container, the seller bends slightly and pours the *meyan* sherbet from another tap. Frequently, the sellers add a little playfulness to this ritual by filling the glass a little, then pulling back and bending again to fill it. These sellers travel along predetermined itineraries every day and have regular customers along these routes. Customers who always buy from the same seller and never patronise a different one are a testament to the continuities and well-established habits involved in the consumption of this traditional drink.

The sherbet is made from the roots of the sassafras *(meyan)* plant. The roots are soaked in water and the juice is collected drop by drop. Each seller makes his own sherbet. For this reason, what is theoretically the same drink can vary considerably in taste from seller to seller: some are stronger, others are softer. Regionally known as *aşlama*, the *meyan* sherbet is kept cold for hours in the special brass containers, which are an indispensable part of this colourful, regional ritual. The sassafras plant grows most abundantly around Halfeti in the southeast and sacks of sassafras roots are sold in regional markets. The roots are shades of brown resembling tree roots. Believed to be a popular remedy for ailments of the stomach and the intestines, many people prepare and brew this beverage themselves at home. For visitors unfamiliar with the local tradition, the taste of the sherbet is likely to be different from anything they know and rather difficult to take in.

A *meyan* sherbet seller

ALL YEAR ROUND

If the sellers of fresh produce and other seasonal items are reminders of the passing of seasons and the cyclical nature of life, these others represent the constancy of particular traditions—that welcome feeling of familiarity in a fast changing world.

While the seasonality of most items, especially fresh fruits and vegetables, gives street food its peculiar charm and authenticity, particular foods have become standard street fare and can be purchased all year round. These are mostly ready-to-eat (or drink) items that street sellers buy from large manufacturers or bakeries to sell to customers in search of a quick and cheap meal. At the top of the list is the *simit* (round sesame bagels), Turkey's street food *par excellence*. Together with a glass of strong tea, *simit* makes a delicious breakfast or an easy afternoon snack in every season and in every part of the country. Other year round street fare include sandwiches, grilled meats, *charcuterie*, candies, Turkish *baklava* and more specific regional items like the *mırra* coffee of the southeast. If the sellers of fresh produce and other seasonal items are reminders of the passing of seasons and the cyclical nature of life, these others represent the constancy of particular traditions—that welcome feeling of familiarity in a fast changing world.

Opposite, clockwise from top left 'Rooster' candy; Apple candy; Simit seller; Turkish *baklava*; Colourful display of charcuterie

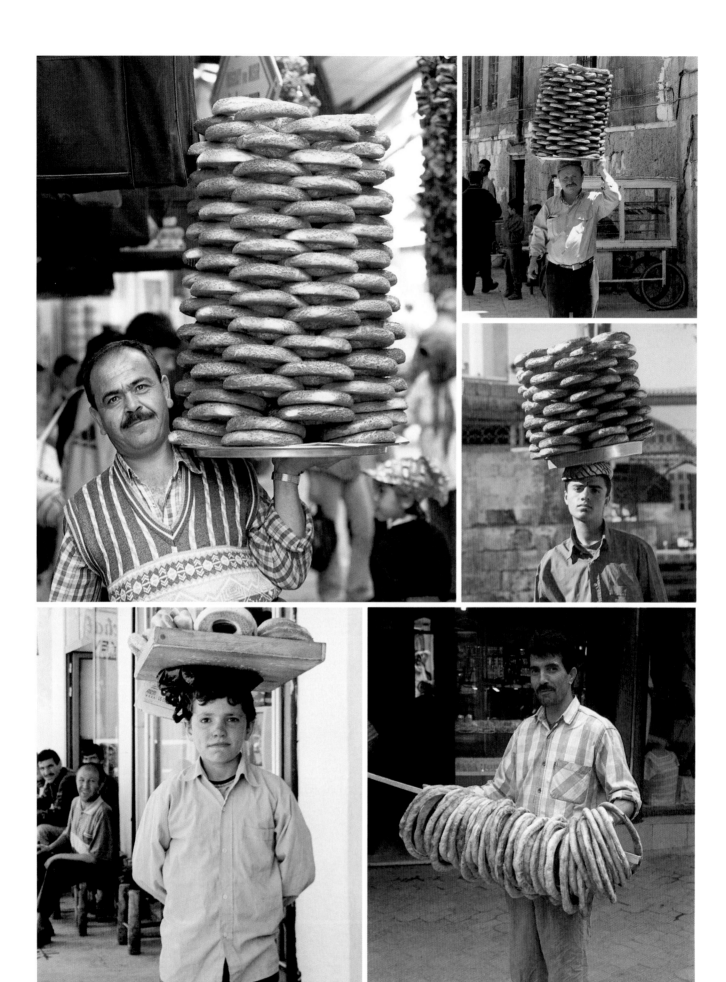

Simit sellers across the country

Picking out a fresh *simit*

SIMIT Sesame Bagels

If Turks living abroad were polled regarding what food they miss most, *simit*, the round sesame bagel, would probably rank quite high in the list. A fresh and crisp *simit* next to a small glass of dark tea with the sea in the background is the classic travel guide image of Istanbul and not without reason. As simple as it seems, *simit* with tea is a cheap but profound culinary experience, especially if accompanied by some cheese and tomatoes. *Simits* are baked daily in neighbourhood bakeries, showing subtle variations that only the seasoned *simit* eaters can trace to particular bakeries: some crispier, some darker brown, some fatter, etc.

Simit sellers of all ages struggle for a living in every season and in every part of the country. Many of them carry the *simits* on a flat tray that they balance on their heads, cushioned by a piece of folded cloth. Others sell them in glass cases mounted on hand-pushed carts. Although wrapping the *simits* in plastic bags is still unheard of, hygiene concerns are causing an increasing number of *simit* sellers to use tongs when handling them. So many *simit* sellers have a good strong voice when they yell out the arrival of *gevrek simit! taze simit!* ("crispy *simits*! fresh *simits*!") that one cannot help wondering whether it is their natural gift or whether their trade inevitably involves some kind of voice training as well.

BREAD *Ekmek*

In the essentially grain-based Turkish culinary culture, bread occupies a central, near sacred status as the basic staple of a large population. To waste bread is a serious offence, even a sin according to some Turks. Enormous quantities of bread are consumed every day across the entire social spectrum and the expression, *ekmek parası kazanmak* ("earning bread money"), is commonly used as a synonym for making a living. The municipal governments regulate the weight and price of bread strictly and not even the poorest member of society goes around without a loaf of bread for the day.

The basic crusty loaf of white bread *(fırancala)* is baked fresh every morning in large 'bread factories' and it is distributed to grocery stores and supermarkets everywhere. Many smaller neighbourhood bakeries still function as well, producing a range of different breads and pastries such as wheat and bran breads that the more health-conscious tend to prefer, *simits* and *poğaças* that are standard breakfast favourites, and the traditional *Ramazan pidesi*, a soft and tasty flat bread baked during the holy month of Ramadan. Although boutique breads have proliferated in fancier supermarkets and gourmet stores in recent years, the freshness, familiar taste and cheapness of the ordinary loaf from the neighbourhood bakery still caters to millions of people.

The primary and indispensable place of bread in Turkish daily life accounts for many well-established practices of purchase and distribution that have been in place since the Ottoman period. In his memoirs of Istanbul in the early 20th century, Hagop Mintzuri, who comes from a family of bakers in the late Ottoman Empire, explains how they used to deliver bread to individual homes and how he helped his father to keep the account books and collect the money at the end of each month.[1] Many neighbourhood grocers still continue the practice of delivering bread every morning or alternatively, the janitors of apartment buildings make their early morning rounds with a basket of fresh loaves. Typically, plastic bags are hung on doorknobs the previous night for this purpose of receiving the bread in the morning. For most Turks, freshly baked, crusty bread is one of the first necessities of the morning ritual, like a cup of tea or the newspaper in other parts of the world.

SANDWICHES *Sandöviç*

The sandwich seller explains how he makes his own sandwiches after buying the bread fresh from the bakery twice a day, first in the early morning and again in the early afternoon. He uses an entire small loaf for each sandwich. He makes some salami and *kaşar* cheese (a kind of cheddar) sandwiches too, but there is always more demand for the feta cheese and tomato sandwiches to which he adds one banana chilli *(carliston biber)* to complete the appetising tricolour scheme. He follows the same route every day and receives bulk orders from offices in the afternoon when he makes most of his business. School children also make good customers. As an international classic of fast street food, cold sandwiches have established a consistent presence in Turkish culinary culture, but far more popular are the grilled sandwiches that are called *"tost"*, sold in small kiosks equipped with a toasting machine.

Clockwise from top right A cheap, quick and appetising lunch; *Pide* bread fresh from the oven at rush hour, Diyarbakır; Bread seller, late 19th century (Istanbul Metropolitan Municipality, Atatürk Library)

WAFER DISCS *Kağıt Helva*

A crisp, cool but sunny winter day! Only a handful of people are outside. The tea gardens of Moda (on the Asian shores of Istanbul), where on a nice day you would be very lucky to find an empty table, are eerily quiet today. Cemal Bey, who sells wafer discs *(kağıt helva)* near the tea garden, lives in Hasanpaşa, a few kilometres away from Moda. On nice sunny days, he comes to Moda; at other times, he remains in Hasanpaşa. He explains that an unwritten code of ethics exists among *kağıt helva* sellers so that none of them trespasses on another's territory for business. Municipal police are always a problem for many of them who do not have the proper licences issued by the municipality, restricting where and how they can sell their wares. Cemal Bey says that in the past, an offer of *kağıt helva* would be an innocent but effective way to get around the municipal police but that no longer does the trick. Nowadays, the police clamp the *kağıt helva* cart and release it only after a hefty fine is paid.

Cemal Bey pushes his cart every day to and from home. It is a formidable distance for the task. He has thought of leaving it in a parking lot but that would cost him a lot of money. "How can I pay for it? I do not make that kind of money", he says. Nonetheless, he is thankful for being able to make a living. With his children grown up, he and his wife are getting by. He says that *helva* used to come in different varieties in the past: sesame-coated ones, ones moulded in different shapes, etc. Nowadays the choices are limited to *kağıt helva* (literally, "paper helva") and *fıstıklı helva*, a sugary, chewy bar with pistachios. The *helvas* keep fresh in plastic bags up to a week. There are two major manufacturers: one on the Anatolian side, the other in "Istanbul" (like the old inhabitants of Istanbul, Cemal Bey reserves the name "Istanbul" for the European side of the city). He has been selling *helva* for 40 years, "since Menderes came" according to his personal calendar (referring to Prime Minister Adnan Menderes who came to power in 1950). Children do not buy as much *helva* as they used to according to Cemal Bey. His customers are mainly adults. The prices may be partly responsible, he reasons: the cost of a *kağıt helva*, about US$0.30 each, is still a lot of money for children with meagre allowances. Changing tastes and habits should not be underestimated either.

He thinks that in this relatively 'genteel' neighbourhood, children probably do not care for these traditional tastes. He also laments that even when children want to buy, parents, out of concern for hygiene, sometimes forbid them to eat anything sold in the streets. Still, for many Turks, *kağıt helva* is associated with happy memories when it used to be eaten during family outings, strolls in parks or by the sea. A more sophisticated way of eating *kağıt helva*, one that even some restaurants have adopted, is with a thick layer of ice cream in between two wafer discs.

From top On a cold and sunny day in Moda, Istanbul; *Kağıt Helva*

Kokoreç on the grill

KOKOREÇ Grilled Lamb Intestines

Perhaps because it is the quintessential food of soccer matches, grilled lamb intestines *(kokoreç)* is a distinctly 'male' food, associated with Istanbul's predominantly male urban crowds. Nowadays, although *kokoreç* carts still show up along soccer stadiums, their numbers are fewer, reflecting the strict regulation of the trade and the fewer number of licences issued by the municipality. Made of lamb intestines, rolls of *kokoreç* rotate on spits over a coal grill, giving out a dense smoke and a strong smell that meat-loving young Turkish men find hard to resist. Slices of grilled *kokoreç* are chopped with a big knife and served with a sprinkle of oregano and paprika on top. With Turkey's pending bid for EU membership, *kokoreç* may soon be banned altogether for hygiene concerns but until then, it continues to provide a cheap and quick lunch to thousands of people every day.

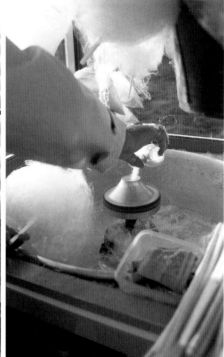

Cotton candy, Gaziantep

ASSORTED CANDY

For many older Turks, the rich varieties of candy that they could purchase in the streets when they were children constitute some of their happiest childhood memories. Today, some of these children's favourites like *macun* (a thick paste of sugar, water and lemon juice plus food colouring to make a rainbow of red, yellow and green that one licks off the tip of a stick), are on the verge of disappearing completely and the occasional *macun* seller is treated as a curiosity. Others like apple candy, cotton candy and lollipops (especially the traditional *horoz şekeri* or 'rooster' candy) have continued to maintain their presence and popularity, albeit with the compulsory use of plastic packaging for reasons of hygiene.

In Gaziantep, we spoke to the Ercan family who make a living selling apple and cotton candy. They moved to Gaziantep after the devastating earthquake of 1999 near Istanbul which killed close to 20,000 people. This is how they prepare the apple candy *(elma şekeri)*: they boil sugar, lemon salt and food colouring until it forms a thick liquid. Apples speared with wooden sticks are then dipped into this liquid, let to cool and solidify on a tray before

being packaged for sale. The typical daily itinerary of Mehmet Ercan covers not just the areas close to schools, but also main streets and public parks. He says that adults are almost as eager to buy the apple candies as children, and on a typical day, he sells 45–50 of them.

For the making of the cotton candy *(pamuk şekeri)*, they use a portable LPG-powered device that they can take to picnics, festivals and open-air gatherings for fresh, on-the-spot cotton candy. Nowadays cotton candy is sold in transparent plastic hoods: they come in pink and white colours—the pink one using a small amount of food colouring. Mehmet Ercan explains that there is no need for concern about calories since one serving of cotton candy has barely a teaspoon of sugar.

The Ercans have two daughters who wish to move to a big city to attend college. They seem to have no interest in continuing the candy business and with a subtle mix of pride and melancholy, Mehmet Ercan points out that he and his wife represent the last generation of a long line of apple and cotton candy makers in their family.

Clockwise from top left *Macun* candy; *Macun* seller, Kemeraltı, Izmir; Assorted candy cart, Ankara; Apple candy, Gaziantep

ŞALGAM Turnip Juice

Şalgam is a sour-tasting, red coloured fermented beverage unique to Adana and its environments in southern Turkey. With the exception of a few very hot months of the summer, it is heavily consumed in the region throughout the entire year. In the streets of Adana, it is sold in containers of different shapes and sizes all day. That some carts are stacked with multiple *şalgam* containers testifies to the high demand on this beverage. These plastic containers are used to replenish the glass display bottles when empty and at the same time, they are sold to customers who want to buy *şalgam* 'in bulk'—especially natives of Adana who have moved to other cities and wish to bring some *şalgam* back with them after visiting their hometown.

The popularity of *şalgam* partly resides in its digestive properties as a result of the fermentation process. In addition to commercial *şalgam*-making, home preparation for personal consumption is quite common in the region. The ingredients are ground bulgur, water, carrots (which give the beverage its red colour), salt, yeast and *şalgam* roots. *Şalgam* root is a light coloured species of the turnip family, known as *brassicarapa* among botanists and as *celem* among the local population of the Adana region. Because it is a rather rare and expensive plant not available every season, the *şalgam* (juice) sold in the streets does not always contain *şalgam* (roots).

To prepare *şalgam*, the ground bulgur is mixed with yeast. The peeled and cleaned carrots are added next, all of them packed into a barrel. In the past, large wooden barrels were used for the procedure, but they have been recently replaced with plastic ones. Water and salt are then added and it is left to ferment for 3–5 days depending on the temperature or the particular time of the year. In winter months when *şalgam* roots are available, these too are added to the carrots, yielding a stronger and somewhat 'spicier' beverage. Because of the yeast used in its preparation, *şalgam* can easily go bad in hot summer months.

As a digestive, refreshing and stomach-comforting beverage, *şalgam* is an indispensable accompaniment to kebabs and heavy meat dishes. It is often served in a glass with a piece of carrot placed in the centre—a presentation known as *tane*.

ISOT Processed Paprika

Processed paprika *(isot)* is a trademark of southeastern cuisine and culture, carried to other parts of the country by migrants from the region. Typically, *isot* is prepared in the households of Urfa during the months of August and September. Long thin paprikas that have turned red in the fields during the summer are handpicked. Their heads, together with the seeds, are removed and spread onto the flat roofs of Urfa houses to dry for one night. The next day, they are packed into plastic bags and left in the sun. Every day, they are taken out, aired for 15–20 minutes and then repacked into the plastic bags, until they darken under the strong southeastern sun. When they are almost black in colour, they are spread on the roof to remove the humidity after which they are ground either by hand or in a grinding machine. It takes 350 kilograms of paprikas to yield about 20 kilograms of *isot*. As the final step, half a kilogram of olive oil is added to every 10 kilograms of *isot*, now ready for use in cooking. *Isot* enters almost every dish in the region and it is an indispensable ingredient of *çiğ köfte* (see page 122). *Isot* is the primary agent for preserving the raw meat and 'cooking' it by long and laborious kneading. For the people of the region, *isot* is a natural addition to every meal. Others who are not used to such spicy food cannot help wondering why anyone would eat such hot food and if it is harmful to the stomach. As hard to believe as it seems, the locals claim that *isot* helps them cope with the heat better. There is indeed a scientific explanation for this claim. Containing volatile oil, piperine and resin, the spice increases the flow of saliva and gastric juices, improves the appetite and if consumed in sufficient quantities, has a cooling effect.[2]

From top *Şalgam* on wheels, Adana; Heaps of *isot* in the market of Gaziantep

Tray of *şam tatlısı*, Adana

ŞAM TATLISI Semolina Dessert

Semir Esen has been selling a kind of semolina dessert (*şam tatlısı*) in the streets of Adana for as long as he can remember. That *şam tatlısı* literally translates as "Damascus dessert" (like *şam fıstığı* translates as "Damascus pistachio") is yet another testimony to the strong cultural and historical connection between southeastern Turkey and Syria, defying the national borders drawn in the early 20th century. Semir Esen is willing to share his recipe for this dessert, but only in very general terms. He is reluctant to give detailed measurements so as "not to reveal trade secrets" as he puts it. He itemises the basic ingredients: semolina, tahini (paste of toasted and ground sesame seeds), sugar and water. Sugar and water are brought to the boil and semolina is added while stirring constantly. It is then removed from the heat and left to thicken after which it is poured onto a flat wide tray. He explains that spreading a thin layer of tahini at the bottom of the tray prevents the dessert from sticking. The rest of the tahini is poured over the dessert, spread neatly and baked. When ready, it is drizzled with a sweet sherbet of sugar and water and decorated with pistachios. Semir Esen explains that his is a year round business and there is no decline in sales even in the summer heat.

BAKLAVA

Baklava is the most famous and internationally acclaimed dessert of the eastern Mediterranean. It is made of paper-thin sheets of filo pastry layered with melted butter and walnuts, after which it is cut into small squares or diamond shapes and baked until golden brown. It is then sweetened with syrup and/or honey. Turkish *baklava* makers feature different varieties of *baklava* filled not only with walnuts (*cevizli baklava*), but with clotted cream (*kaymaklı baklava*) and pistachios (*fıstıklı baklava*), the latter being the culinary pride of the southeast (Gaziantep in particular), Turkey's pistachio region. Although most of the *baklava* consumed in major Turkish cities is bought from traditional establishments of southeastern origin like Güllüoğlu, there are literally hundreds of *baklava* makers and equally many street sellers of *baklava* throughout Turkey. Among the numerous flour-based syrupy desserts of Turkish cuisine, *baklava* undoubtedly ranks a royal top with a considerable history behind it. Historians record that among the desserts produced in the imperial kitchens of the Ottoman Palace, *baklava* was among the few very special items always present in every festive occasion, especially religious holidays *(bayrams)* and the breaking of fast *(iftar)* during the holy month of Ramadan.[3]

Young *baklava* seller, Gaziantep

MIRRA Southeastern Coffee

A specialty of southeastern Turkey, *mirra* is a thick coffee consumed in very small amounts. The coffee beans are ground in special wooden mills and the coffee is boiled for hours until it reaches the consistency of molasses. Cardamom is added to give the coffee a distinctive aroma.

The serving of mirra is a very colourful and interesting local ritual. It is served in mini porcelain glasses with no handles. The glasses are filled twice and you are expected to finish it in two gulps. Once finished, you are not supposed to put the glass on the table but rather, hand it back to the person who is serving. This is believed to bring good luck, and strict observation of the custom is expected!

A coffee house in Gaziantep

Clockwise from top The *mırra* ceremony, Urfa; Pouring the *mırra*, Urfa; Itinerant coffee seller, late 19th century (Istanbul Metropolitan Municipality, Atatürk Library)

ENDNOTES

INTRODUCTION

1 Robert Mantran, *17. Yüzyılın Ikinci Yarısında Istanbul*, Ankara: Türk Tarih Kurumu Basımevi, 1990: 167–169

2 Reşat Ekrem Koçu, *Tarihte Istanbul Esnafı*, Istanbul: Doğan Kitap, 2002: 188

3 Robert Mantran, *17. Yüzyılın Ikinci Yarısında Istanbul*, Ankara: Türk Tarih Kurumu Basımevi, 1990: 311–323

4 Reşat Ekrem Koçu, *Tarihte Istanbul Esnafı*, Istanbul: Doğan Kitap, 2002: 212–214

5 Cited in Robert Mantran, *17. Yüzyılın Ikinci Yarışında Istanbul*, Ankara: Türk Tarih Kurumu Basımevi, 1990: 312

6 In his account of everyday life in Istanbul between 1897 and 1940, Hagop Mintzuri writes that women did not go to the butcher or the grocery store. He also mentions that bread was delivered to homes from neighbourhood bakeries regularly, keeping a debit account for each household for weekly or monthly payments. (See Hagop Mintzuri, *Istanbul Anıları 1897–1940*, Istanbul: Tarih Vakfı Yurt Yayınları, 1998: 26–27)

7 Some recent English titles focusing on Turkish cuisine are Joan and David Peterson, *Eat Smart in Turkey*, Gingko Press Inc., 1996; Hüseyin Özer, *Sofra Cookbook: Modern Turkish and Middle Eastern Cookery*, London: Thorsons, 1998; *Timeless Tastes, Turkish Culinary Culture*. Istanbul: Vehbi Koç Vakfı Publications, Istanbul: MAS Matbaacılık A.Ş., 1999; Mehmet Gürs, *Downtown Cookbook*, Istanbul: MAS Matbaacılık A.Ş., 2000 and *Imperial Taste: 700 Years of Culinary Culture*. Turkish Ministry of Culture Publication, Ankara: Plaka Matbaacılık A.Ş., 2000

WINTER

1 John Fedor, *Reader's Digest Organic Gardening for the 21ˢᵗ Century*, New York: Reader's Digest, 2001: 249

2 John Ayto, *A Gourmet's Guide: Food and Drink from A to Z*, Oxford: Oxford University Press, 1994: 284

3 From Ramazan Albay, "Bursa'dan Damağa Vurgular" in M. Sabri Koz ed. *Yemek Kitabı*, Istanbul: Kitabevi, 2002: 370

4 John Ayto, *A Gourmet's Guide, Food and Drink from A to Z*, Oxford: Oxford University Press, 1994.

5 The 18th century Ottoman poet Nedim mentions the "*helva* conversations" of Sultan Ahmet III and his grand vizier Damat Ibrahim Paşa, for which he specially composed seven long poems in the *kaside* genre. Cited in Abdülbaki Gölpınarlı ed. *Nedim Divanı*, Istanbul: Inkilap ve Aka Kitabevi, 1972: 97–110

6 J.Freely, *Evliya Çelebi'nin Istanbulu*, Istanbul: Yapı Kredi Yayınları, 2003: 92–93

7 Murat Belge, *Tarih Boyunca Yemek Kültürü*, Istanbul: Iletişim Yayınları, 2001: 211

8 Murat Belge, *Tarih Boyunca Yemek Kültürü*, Istanbul: Iletişim Yayınları, 2001: 38

9 Albert Sonnenfeld ed. *Food: A Culinary History from Antiquity to the Present*, New York: Penguin Books, 2000: 357

10 Murat Belge, *Tarih Boyunca Yemek Kültürü*, Istanbul: Iletişim Yayınları, 2001: 40

11 Cited in Andy Footner, "Salep and Boza" in *Time Out Istanbul*, February 2002, n.2: 34

SPRING

1 Ayşe Baysal, "Türk Mutfağında Köfte, Sarma ve Dolmalar: Türleri, Özellikleri, Besin Değerleri" in M. Sabri Koz ed. *Yemek Kitabı*, Istanbul: Kitabevi, 2002: 201–207

2 H. Necdet Islı, "Kadirihane'de Aşure", M.Sabri Koz, ed. *Yemek Kitabı*, Istanbul: Kitabevi, 2002: 719

3 H. Necdet Islı, ibid.: 721

4 Nejat Sefercioğlu, *Türk Yemekleri: 18. Yuzyıla ait yazma bir yemek risalesi*. Ankara: Kültür ve Turizm Bakanlığı Yayınları, 1985: 75–80

5 Hagop Mintzuri, *Istanbul Anıları*, Istanbul: Tarih Vakfı Yurt Yayınları, 1998: 34

6 Eren Akçiçek, "Dünden Bugüne Şerbetçiliğimiz", *Yemek Kitabı*. Istanbul: Kitabevi, 2002: 762

SUMMER

1 Çiğdem Öztürkçine Erduran and Ömer Faruk Şerifoğlu, "Anadolu'da Patlıcan Kültürü ve Yemekleri" in M. Sabri Koz ed. *Yemek Kitabı*, Istanbul: Kitabevi, 2002: 261–264

2 Ali Rıza Bey, "Osmanlı Hayatında Kadınlar", *Tarih ve Edebiyat Mecmuası*, v.5, n.17, 1981: 32–37

3 Cited in Artun Ünsal, "Osmanlı Mutfağı" in M. Sabri Koz ed. *Yemek Kitabı*, Istanbul: Kitabevi, 2002: 91

4 Cited in Murat Belge, *Tarih Boyunca Yemek Kültürü*, Istanbul: Iletişim, 2001: 70

5 Nail Tan and Özdemir Tan, "Kastamonu'da Doğada Kendiliğinden Yetişen Bitki ve Meyvelerle Beslenme" in M. Sabri Koz ed. *Yemek Kitabı* Istanbul: Kitabevi, 2002: 540

AUTUMN

1 Cited in Artun Ünsal, *Ölmez Ağacın Peşinde: Türkiye'de Zeytin ve Zeytinyağı*, Istanbul: Yapı ve Kredi Bankası Yayınları, 2000: 8

2 Alan Davidson, *The Penguin Companion to Food*, London: Penguin Books, 2002: 661

3 Esma Şimşek, "Osmaniye Mutfağı ve Mahalli Yemekler", in M. Sabri Koz ed., *Yemek Kitabı*, Istanbul: Kitabevi, 2002: 454

4 Dr. Yaşar Kalafat, "Türkmen Dünyası Beslenme Kültüründe Bereket Motifi", *Türk Mutfak Kültürü Üzerine Araştırmalar*. Ankara: Türk Halk Kültürünü Araştırma ve Tanıtma Vakfı, 1999: 139–140

5 A. Süheyl Ünver, *Istanbul Risaleleri*, No.5, Istanbul: Büyükşehir Belediyesi Kültür Işleri Daire Başkanlığı Yayınları, 1996: 83

ALL YEAR ROUND

1 Hagop Mintzuri, *Istanbul Anıları 1897–1940*, Istanbul: Tarih Vakfı Yurt Yayınları, 1998

2 Alan Davidson, *The Penguin Companion to Food*, London: Penguin Books, 2002: 713–714

3 Arif Bilgin, "Seçkin Mekanda Seçkin Damaklar: Osmanlı Sarayında Beslenme Alışkanlıkları, 15–17. Yüzyıl", M. Sabri Koz ed. *Yemek Kitabı*, Istanbul: Kitabevi, 2002: 60

SELECTED BIBLIOGRAPHY

AYTO, John, *A Gourmet's Guide: Food and Drink from A to Z*, Oxford: Oxford University Press, 1994

BELGE, Murat, *Tarih Boyunca Yemek Kültürü*, Istanbul: Iletişim Yayınları, 2001

ÇEVIK, Nihal Kadıoğlu, ed., *Imperial Taste: 700 Years of Culinary Culture*, Ankara: Republic of Turkey Ministry of Culture, 2000

DAVIDSON, Alan, *The Penguin Companion to Food*, London: Penguin Books, 2002

DELEON, Jak, *Eski Istanbul'un Yaşayan Tadı*, Istanbul: Remzi Kitabevi, 1995

EKSEN, Ilhan, *Çokkültürlü Istanbul Mutfağı*, Istanbul: Sel Yayıncılık, 2001

EVREN, Burçak, *Ottoman Craftsmen and Their Guilds*, Istanbul: Doğan Kitapçılık A.Ş., 1999

FEDOR, John, *Reader's Digest Organic Gardening for the 21st Century*, New York: Reader's Digest, 2001

FREELY, John, *Evliya Çelebi'nin Istanbul'u*, Çev: Müfit Günay, Istanbul: Yapı Kredi Yayınları, 2003

KOÇU, Reşad Ekrem, *Tarihte Istanbul Esnafı*, Istanbul: Doğan Kitapçılık A.Ş., 2002

KOZ, M. Sabri, *Yemek Kitabı: Tarih, Halkbilimi, Edebiyat*, Istanbul: Kitabevi, 2002

MANTRAN, Robert, *17inci Yüzyılın Ikinci Yarısında Istanbul*, I. Cilt, Çev: Mehmet Ali Kılıçbay, Enver Özcan, Ankara: Türk Tarih Kurumu Basımevi, 1990

MINTZURI, Hagop, *Istanbul Anıları 1897–1940*, Istanbul: Tarih Vakfı Yurt Yayınları, 1998

SONNENFELD, Albert ed. *Food: A Culinary History from Antiquity to the Present*, London: Penguin Books, 2000

SUNAR, Engin, *Balık Yemekleri*, Istanbul: Say Yayınları, 2002

TOYGAR, Kamil ed., *Türk Mutfak Kültürü Üzerine Araştırmalar*, Ankara: Türk Halk Kültürünü Araştırma ve Tanıtma Vakfı, Yayın No: 23, 1999

ÜNSAL, Artun, *Ölmez Ağacın Peşinde: Türkiye'de Zeytin ve Zeytinyağı*, Istanbul: Yapı Kredi Yayınları, 2000

ÜNSAL, Ayfer T., *Ayıntab'tan Gaziantep'e Yeme Içme*, Istanbul: Iletişim Yayınları, 2002

ÜNVER, Süheyl, *Istanbul Risaleleri*, Cilt 3, Istanbul: Büyükşehir Belediyesi Kültür Işleri Daire Başkanlığı Yayınları, No: 19, 1999

WOODWARD, Sarah, *The Ottoman Kitchen*, New York: Interlink Books, 2001

YERASIMOS, Marianna, *Osmanlı Mutfağı*, Istanbul: Boyut Yayıncılık, 2002

INDEX

INDEX OF RECIPES